FRANK LLOYD WRIGHT: REBEL IN CONCRETE

By the author of
AMERICAN WOMEN WHO SCORED FIRSTS

FRANK LLOYD WRIGHT

REBEL IN CONCRETE

By Aylesa Forsee

MACRAE SMITH COMPANY: PHILADELPHIA

The author and publisher wish to thank the following for permission to reproduce photographs in this book: Mr. Wayne Andrews, Brooklyn, New York, pp. 47, 84, 87, 113, 123, 129, 135, 140, 147; Beth Sholom Synagogue, Philadelphia, Pennsylvania (Jacob Stelman, photographer), p. 169; Florida Southern College, Lakeland, Florida (Paul Wille, photographer), p. 137; S. C. Johnson and Son, Inc., Racine, Wisconsin, pp. 117, 149; The Museum of Modern Art, New York City, pp. 53, 56, 64, 78; Palmer Pictures, San Francisco, California, p. 81; H. C. Price Company, Bartlesville, Oklahoma (Joe D. Price, photographer), p. 162; Mr. William H. Short, New York City, p. 155.

CONTENTS

LIST OF ILLUSTRATIONS

Frontispiece drawing of Frank Lloyd Wright by Guy Fry

FRANK LLOYD WRIGHT: REBEL IN CONCRETE

1
ADVENTURES MAKE STRONG MEN

ONE SUMMER DAY IN THE 1880'S A TEEN-AGE BOY WITH DARK, bushy hair strode energetically along the edge of the State Capitol grounds at Madison, Wisconsin. His thoughts were suddenly interrupted by the crash and tumble of bricks and timbers. Turning toward the capitol he saw clouds of lime dust puffing out through the window openings of the west wing, then under construction. From a basement doorway laborers with bloodstained faces plunged headlong, dodging beams that were still falling.

Transfixed by horror, the youthful Frank Lloyd Wright realized that although the walls of the building were still standing, the roof and floors had collapsed, hurling the workmen into the basement. From the wreckage came moans and groans of those buried beneath it. Firemen arrived and directed the efforts of volunteer rescuers who were pawing frantically at beams, bricks, and plaster. Hour after hour they brought out mangled men and laid them on the grass whitened by lime. Most of the forty workmen were dead.

That night dreams of death and destruction troubled Frank's sleep. For days he relived the tragic scene. What had happened to make the building collapse, he kept asking himself. Was the whole thing a sham? Later, official investigation revealed that the contractor had filled the hearts of the piers with broken brick and stone under the impression that what went inside didn't matter. Defective at the core, they had let down the columns supporting floors and roof.

Frank, who from his earliest years had been interested in architecture, vowed that anything he built would be solid and genuine.

Many things in Frank Lloyd Wright's early life seemed to influence him toward becoming an architect. Even before his birth on June 8, 1869, at Richland Center, Wisconsin, his mother Anna Lloyd-Jones Wright had made up her mind that if she ever had a son he would build beautiful things.

A woman of fire and energy, Mrs. Wright was the daughter of Richard Lloyd-Jones, Welsh hatter and Unitarian minister who had migrated to Wisconsin. Fascinated by buildings, she saw to it that Timothy Cole engravings of English cathedrals graced the walls of her son's bedroom in the modest Wright home.

Frank's musically gifted father, William Russell Cary Wright, came from the same family of intellectuals as the poet, James Russell Lowell. Amherst-educated, he had studied medicine and law in turn and then, abandoning both, moved to Wisconsin, where he became simultaneously an itinerant minister and a musician. Frank was his first child; the second was a daughter named Jane.

When Frank was only three, Mr. Wright was called to a church at Weymouth, an elm-shaded village near Boston. The third Wright baby, a girl born in the gray wooden parsonage, was named Maginel. Mrs. Wright, who loved nature, often took the children on hikes through the fields and woodlands around Weymouth. Wearing a blue cape with brass buttons and walking with a free stride, she pointed out the ferns, flowers, and animals that she knew.

At the age of six Frank went to a private school, but because he preferred to do things that were the product of his own imagination, he gained little from formal education. Mrs. Wright, who had been a country schoolteacher in Wisconsin, supplemented his schooling, and a friend of hers taught Frank to draw and paint— activities he liked enormously.

His father, whom Frank both loved and feared, supervised the musical education of the children. When Frank made too many mistakes while playing the Steinway square piano, the nervously impatient Mr. Wright would rap him on the knuckles—but this didn't keep Frank from loving music. Nights he often lay on his bed listening to his father play Bach or Beethoven. Bach, he thought, must have composed on bright days because there was sunshine in his music.

As soon as Frank was old enough he learned to pump the church organ while his father practiced. Alone in the gloomy chamber behind the organ that was lighted by an oil lamp, he kept his eyes on a lead marker that indicated air pressure. Fortissimo passages required pumping the bellows vigorously by means of a projecting lever handle. Occasionally the beauty of sound would enchant him and he would almost forget to pump. But during some practice sessions Mr. Wright played so long that Frank, with aching back and arms, would wonder if his father remembered where the breath for the organ was coming from. When the music stopped cascading forth, his father would appear, and they would walk home hand in hand.

There was never much money in the parsonage, but the house was saved from drabness by Mrs. Wright's appreciation of the beauty of simple things. Her artistry in selecting a print in a maple frame or arranging flowers or seasonal foliage helped the children to learn to discriminate between what was good and what was inferior.

The ingredients of Mrs. Wright's recipes for child rearing were clean living, high thinking, and plain cooking—too plain at times to suit Frank. Although his mother's graham bread, porridge, and roasted meats were nourishing and palatable, he yearned for pie, cake and store candy.

Mrs. Wright continually sought means to develop the resources and qualities Frank would need as an architect. At the Philadelphia Centennial Exposition in 1876 she saw an exhibition of toys prescribed by a German educator, Friedrich Froebel, to develop feeling for basic form, materials and color. These toys, called "gifts," consisted of smooth maple blocks, cubes, spheres, and triangles with which to build. There were also straight, slender sticks, dried peas, pieces of cardboard and glazed papers of yellow, scarlet, blue, and green for creating designs.

Although the toys were designed for kindergarten children and Frank was now seven, Mrs. Wright saw their possibilities for a boy destined to become an architect. She not only purchased the gifts in Boston, but also took lessons in the Froebel method, and then came home and taught the children. Frank was fascinated. Not content to follow prescribed structures, his inventive mind created new combinations. These increased his natural sensitivity to color and awareness of geometric forms in nature.

Absorbed in the new materials, Frank often ignored the childish games indulged in by Jane and Maginel. But evenings the family enjoyed reading or making music together. Attracted by Mrs. Wright's charm and Mr. Wright's ability for stimulating conversation, distinguished visitors came frequently. Frank's father, who had been a Baptist before he became a Unitarian minister, had much to say about the beauty of truth and the unity of all things. Family recreation was not always on such a high intellectual plane, however; occasionally they went on an outing to Nantucket or a clam bake at Narragansett.

The year Frank was eleven the family moved to Madison, Wisconsin, where Mr. Wright set up a conservatory of music in quarters over a store building. On Lake Mendota the Wrights found a brown wooden house that suited them. Pleased with his assignment to an attic bedroom, Frank lettered SANCTUM on his flat wooden door that opened with a latch and string.

One day in late spring Frank's Uncle James, a tall, bearded man with laugh wrinkles at the corners of his eyes, drove in from the "Valley" with a cow to provide milk for the frail Maginel. The Valley, which was close to Spring Green and only forty miles from Madison, was the home of Mrs. Wright's parents and her brothers James, Thomas, Enos and John, who owned many acres of adjacent farmland. After some discussion it was decided that Frank should go home with him to work for the summer.

The prospect was an exciting one for Frank. There would be all the outdoors to explore with his cousins on neighboring farms. He liked witty, vigorous Uncle James and his Welsh grandfather, who could tell wonderful stories about his early days in Wisconsin when Indians lived in the neighborhood. But as Uncle James' team of horses clopped off toward the Valley, Frank's mind was filled with thoughts of his mother and home. Every turn of the wheels of the creaking wagon was carrying him away from familiar sights, sounds, and companions.

As they came within sight of the Valley, Frank caught his breath at the beauty of a shimmering stream and the northern hill slopes forested with balm of Gilead trees and Lombardy poplars. All the uncles' farms looked prosperous, with large fields and barns.

At Uncle James' Frank was a little disappointed in Aunt Laura, who was much less gentle than his mother—and his mother would not have approved of the supper with fried potatoes and fried meat. But he felt at home in the whitewashed attic bedroom with a stovepipe running through it from the room below.

Tired from the trip, Frank went to bed early, but he was hardly asleep, it seemed, when an explosive banging on the stovepipe startled him. Then he heard his uncle's voice. "Four o'clock, my boy. Time to get up."

Shivering, Frank stumbled toward a chair on which Aunt Laura had laid a hickory shirt and blue jean overalls. The socks were so coarse, the cowhide shoes so stiff, that he decided to discard them in favor of bare feet.

As soon as Frank was downstairs Uncle James took him to the cow stable roofed with straw. Milking, with the overpowering smell of the barn, was harder than he'd imagined. The breakfast that followed was unlike any Frank had ever eaten—pancakes, sorghum, fried pork, cornmeal mush and milk.

After breakfast Frank helped Aunt Laura feed the calves by holding his fingers in a pail of milk and letting the calves suck them.

"Now that you've finished that, you can haul some sticks of wood over to the cross-cut saw," Uncle James directed.

The dinner eaten at noon was a hearty one, but Frank would have eaten even more had he known he'd be working so hard, he thought later, as he pulled out a splinter he'd got in his finger while helping Uncle James build a fence. Back at the house Aunt Laura wanted several pails of water, which Frank carried from a pump in the yard, and then the cows, which had been turned out in open pasture, had to be rounded up.

Frank had barely swallowed his last bite of supper when Uncle James pushed his chair away from the table. "We must milk the cows, boy," he said.

"Again?" Frank questioned.

By seven thirty he was almost too tired to climb up to his attic bedroom. The soles of his feet were punctured and stone-bruised and his big toe throbbed from repeated stubbing. Stiff and sore, he lay thinking about home and longing for September to come.

The next thing he was conscious of was the annoying staccato beat on the stovepipe.

That day and the ones that followed, Frank was involved in never-ending chores. He was expected to feed the chickens, hunt for eggs, and carry feed to the pigs and boars that had ugly tusks and foamed at the mouth. Twice a day the cows had to be milked and herded to and from the pasture. They had a way of wandering off until the only clue to their whereabouts was the faraway tinkle of a cowbell. Sometimes it was after dark before Frank found them; sometimes he didn't find them at all and had to enlist help.

Then there was always the garden. Why did weeds grow so much more readily than the carrots, lettuce, or onions, he would ask himself, crossly yanking up ragweed, dock or quack grass—and if it wasn't weeds it was invasion by worms, insects, or inquisitive pigs. Uncle James was wise and kind and laughed a lot, but would not tolerate laziness, vulgarity, or dishonesty.

One morning, rebellion at the back-breaking toil coupled with a longing to see his family prompted Frank to run away. Determinedly he struck off across the hills toward the Wisconsin River, where a ferryboat ran. Because he was actually very fond of Uncle James, Frank couldn't avoid feeling guilty about leaving in this way—but then he remembered the cows, the pigs and the garden.

His timing had been perfect: the ferryboat was at the dock. Waiting for the boat to start, Frank sat on the edge of it dangling his dusty, weary feet in the water and enjoying the coolness. He looked up curiously when a long-bearded man came down the riverbank toward the boat. When Frank saw it was Uncle Enos his heart skipped a beat.

Uncle Enos, his mother's youngest brother, had been kind to Frank, sometimes wrestling with him in a friendly way, but what would he say or do now?

"Where are you going, Frank?" Uncle Enos asked in a matter-of-fact voice.

Dismay at the abrupt termination of his adventure brought tears to Frank's eyes, and he couldn't find his voice to answer his uncle's question.

Without a word Uncle Enos came to his side and led him to the riverbank. Seated beside his uncle, who was a solid, substantial person, Frank clutched at the grass spasmodically while pouring out his homesickness and resentment. Uncle Enos' dark eyes and voice were sympathetic, but as he talked with Frank he tried to get him to see that if he kept at the chores he'd become strong. Work, he said, was really an adventure. In response to Frank's outburst about Aunt Laura's crossness, Uncle Enos pointed out that she wasn't well and that both she and Uncle James would be unhappy if Frank carried out his plan.

Remorsefully Frank returned to Uncle James' and under a protective shield of darkness climbed to the room in the attic. Next morning Aunt Laura and Uncle James acted as if nothing had happened.

Frank tried to develop muscles, and tried to see work as an adventure; but the tasks still seemed too hard and too numerous, and Uncle James had no patience with work half done. On nights when he couldn't sleep Frank would go outside and with dew-wet grass tickling his feet climb the stony hill behind the house and sit listening to the songs of summer insects that made him yearn to hear his father's music. With mysterious shadows around him he would dream of the great deeds he meant to perform.

On a day when the grind of chores was irksome and everything went wrong, Frank ran away again. After he was brought back by Uncle James, he hid in a strawstack as a protest, but unintentionally fell asleep there and slept all night. He was very much ashamed when he awakened next morning and found he had caused great anxiety. Never again would he run away, he resolved, and he'd work harder than he ever had before.

Frank learned how to cope with weeds, nettles, briars and poison ivy. Balancing on a one-legged stool, he became an expert milker. Chores connected with the cows became much less tedious after he discovered that the animals had some almost human traits.

Frank's mother had trained him to see, to feel, and to listen. Now he began to appreciate the opportunities the farm offered for the use of these faculties. He watched the flights of birds and learned their calls, and paused occasionally to revel in the feel of moss under his bare feet, sniff at the heavy scent of clover, or savor the flavor of a wild strawberry on his tongue. He could rejoice in the colors of a sunset or the star-shaped flame of a lily.

When or how it happened Frank could not have said, but his muscles strengthened and his blisters and aches disappeared. Uncle Enos had said work was an adventure that made strong men and finished weak ones. Work was not yet an adventure for Frank, but he could see it might be when one was fit for it. He'd be one of the strong ones.

2 *PUSHED INTO MANHOOD*

FRANK LIKED THE RELAXED TEMPO OF SUNDAYS IN THE VALLEY.
Customarily he went with Aunt Laura and Uncle James to the
brown wooden chapel built by his Lloyd-Jones uncles and grandfather. Around the pulpit covered with a purple velvet cloth and
flanked by wild flowers gathered by Frank and his cousins, sat
perhaps seventy-five persons—most of them relatives, although
neighbors and hired help were welcome to attend. For the older
ones rockers were provided.

Frank's grandfather, aunts and uncles, all Unitarians, took
turns preaching and had much to say about Truth and, "This is
the way; walk ye in it." Stalwart, white-bearded Grandfather read
the Bible with a strong Welsh accent and delivered sermons with
such fervor that he reminded Frank of the prophet Isaiah. But
Uncle Jenkin from Chicago was the one who could always be
depended upon to stir the emotions of his audience.

Frequently after the church service there would be a picnic,
with food set out on the pine tables in the grove of trees that mild,
poetic Uncle Thomas had planted around the chapel. Occasionally, to celebrate a birthday or to lend festivity to a foray for wild
strawberries, plums, grapes, or puckery red-black chokecherries,
the Lloyd-Jones clan went on an all-day picnic, their wagons
moving off in a procession to a grassy site near spring or stream.
There were times when Frank's family came from Madison to
share the fun.

The uncles hung swings for the children under trees with the sun coming aslant through the leaves. If they were near a stream free from water moccasins, they waded, swam and watched catkins cutting circles on the surface. After playing games awhile, they could all hardly wait to sample the food the aunts had spread out on bright-colored cloths on the grass—Dutch rolls, roast pig, chicken, baked ham, hard-boiled eggs, fresh vegetables, cheese, preserves, turnovers, pies, doughnuts, seasonal fruits, and layer cakes. After a huge meal, everyone sang. When Frank's father was there he conducted hymns or accompanied on his violin the Welsh songs the oldsters knew, and sometimes Frank and his cousins recited pieces they had memorized.

In addition to picnics there was always much visiting back and forth. For weddings or camp meetings the whole countryside turned out. Even when left to his own resources, Frank learned to sandwich in some entertainment between chores. In the stream of spring water flowing below the house he squished mud up between his toes, built dams and sailed make-believe boats. Lying on his stomach he studied ants, beetles, tumblebugs, garter snakes, toads, and turtles whose color patterns and movements delighted him. Sometimes when it rained, Frank supplemented his Saturday night bath—for which water had to be carried from the cistern and heated on the range—by shucking his clothes and running outside into the downpour.

By August, when rows of yellow grain sheaves marched across the tawny stubble, Frank was finding the routines rather to his liking—not that there weren't still problems. Farm life demanded initiative, versatility, common sense. At times he was threatened by hoofs and horns and plagued by stings and bites. There was the day when the heavy-necked, bellowing bull chased him, and another day when the kindly cow named Spot broke into the granary, ate her fill, drank all the water she wanted, and died. And when sullen clouds hurled thunderbolts or lightning cracked above wind-lashed trees, Frank wished for the security of his home beside the blue waters of Lake Mendota.

September, long awaited, finally came. He'd learned a lot, thought Frank, riding beside Uncle James toward Madison, where the dome of the capitol shone white in the sun. His fingers were quick, he could work almost as hard as a man, and he wasn't afraid of anything—well, maybe a little afraid of storms and of people. Buoyantly he bounded up the steps at home and flung his arms around his mother. Turning to Jane and Maginel he exclaimed, "How you've grown!"

On the day he approached the forbidding brick structure with beetle-browed windows known as the Second Ward School, Frank was much less sure of himself. Because he'd spent the summer on the farm he had no companions with whom he might share his foray into the unknown.

On the playground a ruckus had erupted. Frank ran to join a circle of boys shouting derisively. The center of their attention was a pile of dead leaves from which emerged the brawny shoulders of a red-haired boy who spluttered angrily.

"What happened?" Frank asked a gangly boy standing beside him.

"Robie's a cripple," the boy explained. "When we tease him he hits us with a crutch. So this time we took his crutches away and then buried him in leaves."

Furious that anyone would take advantage of a handicapped person, Frank ran over to where the crutches lay and picked them up.

Toughened by his summer's experiences, Frank turned on the gang and advanced menacingly. The tormentors took to their heels.

Although Robie Lamp was older, Frank so admired his courage and resourcefulness that they became friends of the heart. Together the boys explored the lake shore and fashioned bows, arrows, and kites with fantastic tails. Jointly they invented an ice boat, a bobsled with double runners, and a water velocipede they christened Frankenrob. On a small printing press in the basement they set type. When a neighbor boy, Charlie Doyon, wanted to join them, the canny partners assented only after persuading Charlie to inveigle two hundred dollars from his wealthy father for purchasing a larger model press and more type. With the acquisition of the press, the boys set up a firm known as Wright, Doyon, and Lamp, Publishers and Printers.

School was less of a challenge to Frank's abilities. He dreaded the monthly ordeal of speaking a piece. On the day when he stood rooted to the platform unable to get beyond the first line of, "Oh sir, I am a widow with children," while his classmates rocked with laughter, he lost the slight confidence he had gained speaking pieces at the Lloyd-Jones picnics. Miserably he glanced toward his teacher, his own Aunt Jane, for comfort. But seeing her flashing black eyes and tight mouth he knew he'd get no help from that quarter. Aunt Jane scorned incompetency. His frustration and humiliation were heightened when at recess mocking playmates chanted, "Oh sir, I am a widow with children." This, on top of the nickname Shaggy which had been fastened on him, was almost more than he could bear.

But at home his woes were forgotten in a welter of activities. Jane, affectionately called Jennie, competed with him in playing the piano. Mr. Wright practiced both violin and piano, composed, sang, and taught Frank how to play the viola.

For evenings of chamber music the family often invited musical friends, including Robie, who took violin lessons from Mr. Wright. Guests were not always amateurs. One famous visitor was Norwegian violinist Ole Bull, in this country on concert tour.

Sometimes singing took the place of playing. Favored composers were Gilbert and Sullivan. After a lusty performance of lyrics from *Mikado* or *Pinafore*, Mr. Wright could be persuaded to play "Pop goes the Weasel." Then Frank's mother served ginger cookies or molasses candy and popcorn.

Another favorite family activity was reading aloud. Their choice of books ranged from *The Arabian Nights* to Ruskin's *Seven Lamps of Architecture* and the poems of Longfellow, Bryant and Whittier. Surreptitiously Frank did a lot of reading on his own from tattered second-hand copies of the Nickel Library available in exchange for a glassie or an aggie or two.

Frank's absent-mindedness as he contemplated the possible outcome of some blood-and-thunder tale usually betrayed him. Then Mrs. Wright, objecting to the mayhem and gun play, would confiscate his latest acquisition, leaving him in suspense over what happened to the outlaws and their victims.

Despite his mother's disapproval of the Nickel Library and her insistence on the use of clean language, Frank was very close to her. His scholarly father inspired no great bond of sympathy, although Frank felt admiration for his intellect and talent. A withdrawn type of person, Mr. Wright often closeted himself to rehearse his sermons or speeches. Then he could be heard pacing back and forth, experimenting with intonation and accent on poems like "The Raven."

Most of the time Frank was too busy with his own projects to pay much attention to his father's. At home and at school he drew and designed. Bridges and dams fascinated him. Reading about the primitive architecture of the Maya, Aztec, and Inca cultures made him yearn to travel to Mexico or Peru to see the remains. It would be exciting to help with the excavations.

Each spring at the end of the school year Frank would return to Uncle James' farm. There he still had to take care of cows, pigs, chickens, and sheep, but he also learned about horses—how to saddle, halter, harness and hitch them. He got thrown off, kicked and bruised, but he ended up riding bareback with great abandon.

It seemed to Frank something was always wrong on the farm. Machinery broke down, calves sickened, hail flattened growing things. People were always saying, "Too wet," or, "Too dry."

At harvest time he was assigned the task of gathering the bundles spewed out by the flashy, horse-drawn reaper and bound by men following the machine. Picking up as many as he could carry at a time, Frank arranged them in piles of eight for the shocker. The sun beat mercilessly on his head, dust irritated his nostrils, the bands on the grain wore his fingernails down to the quick, but there was satisfaction in being counted as part of a work crew.

One hot day Frank sat down on a bundle of grain to rest a moment. Refreshed by the inaction and a drink from a jug of spring water, he wiped the sweat from his brow and leaned over to pick up the bundle on which he'd been sitting. He had a curious sensation when something slithered out of the bundle: there lay a rattlesnake coiled in the stubble. For a second Frank stood fascinated by the brown and gold pattern on its body. Then the snake rattled ominously.

Leaping out of its range, Frank seized a three-tined pitchfork that had been left beside the jug of water. With a vicious jab he pinned the rattler to the ground, and then, using the water jug for a hammer, he flattened the head of the writhing reptile. He was gloating over the nine rattles when the reaper came opposite him and Uncle James got down from the seat. Frank expected to be commended for his bravery. Instead Uncle James asked, "Why didn't you get help?"

"Why?" Frank replied.

"Why? You are barefooted. You might get worse than hurt."

That summer and succeeding ones Frank added more and more to his farming skills. By the time he was fourteen he was doing a man's work and being paid for it. Besides, his experiences had given him self-reliance and courage. Repeatedly witnessing the inevitability of sunshine after rain had fostered an optimistic spirit—and the Lloyd-Jones uncles had instilled in him some of their own simplicity, strength, sense of humor and insight.

Frank needed these qualities to face the situation at home. His father, discouraged by the fact that the conservatory was not paying off, had taken refuge in moodiness and impracticality. The aunts and uncles were willing to help out, but their offers hurt his pride. Immersed in the study of Sanskrit, he became waspish whenever the subject of finances was introduced.

Although his mother remained outwardly serene and cheerful, Frank could see the habitual anxiety in her dark brown eyes. More and more she turned to him for advice and companionship.

About this time Frank read a chapter in Victor Hugo's *Notre Dame* which impressed him. In it Hugo declared that the Renaissance had actually been a setting sun instead of a dawn, and that the great mother-art, architecture, so long formalized, would come spiritually alive again in the latter part of the nineteenth or early twentieth century. I'll help bring it alive, thought Frank, tingling with expectancy.

But when at sixteen he was ready for college, he wondered where the money was coming from to give him the training he'd need as an architect. His father's earnings, small at best, had shrunk even more. Maginel was sickly, and Mrs. Wright was los-ing her vitality. Frank suspected that in her efforts to economize she wasn't eating enough.

One day when the situation had become unendurable, Frank's mother suggested that Mr. Wright leave. Although her voice was quiet and controlled, Frank sensed the heartbreak back of her words.

Mr. Wright disappeared completely. No letters came back, no communication of any kind. In Frank's mind revolved the nagging question as to whether his father had ever really loved him or other members of the family. And he couldn't push down feelings of injustice and resentment over privations the family was now subjected to.

Getting a college education had appeared doubtful even before his father left. Now it looked completely impossible. Furthermore, he was faced with the responsibilities of becoming the head of the family—forced into manhood, he thought bitterly.

3 COMPANIONED BY DREAMS

WHEN FALL CAME, FRANK DID NOT WANT TO ENTER THE UNIVERSITY of Wisconsin at Madison because there was no school of architecture, but he lacked money to go elsewhere. Mrs. Wright, who had a passionate respect for education, persuaded him to enroll in Civil Engineering. To help out with the family income, Frank got a job as assistant in the office of Allen D. Conover, Dean of Engineering, and was paid thirty-five dollars a month.

Each morning Frank walked to the University, which was two miles from home. What he learned in the classroom seemed inappropriate to his goals in architecture. Dissatisfied and impatient, he had the feeling that he was merely marking time. He rather liked mathematics, taught by an academic little man with sideburns, but English was a big disappointment. He yearned for added proficiency in writing, but his instructor did little more than correct glaring grammatical errors.

At noon Frank would report to Conover's office, where he ate the lunch his mother had packed for him and then spent the afternoon at the drawing board. Experiences in Conover's office were not very challenging. The cultivated, kindhearted dean took a personal interest in Frank, and whenever possible gave him opportunities for actual construction, but there weren't many. And although Conover was sound as an engineer, he was not imaginative as an architect.

Frank's social life was as frustrating as his collegiate one. The attitude of the Lloyd-Jones relatives and of many Madisonites that his father's desertion had been a disgrace intensified his shyness and made him a little distrustful of people. Because he turned most of the money he earned over to his mother, he had little to spend on recreation or on girls. He did pledge Phi Delta Theta, but the activities of the fraternity were on a very modest scale. Although his friend Robie Lamp was no longer in school, Frank and he still had projects. But Frank spent most of his evenings studying or reading Carlyle, Goethe, Shelley, and William Blake. Under the impression that it was unmanly, he had given up music. He bypassed collegiate sports but did box occasionally.

When the Freshman party came along, a friend arranged a date for Frank. Arraying himself in a black suit, white tie, and narrow patent leather shoes, he rented a carriage and called for May White at Ladies' Hall. The evening was a series of blunders, and Frank seemed unable to come up with appropriate comments.

Thinking it was what he was expected to do, Frank had planned to give May a goodnight kiss when he got her back to Ladies' Hall, but he was so flustered that all he could do was blurt out, "Thank you," after which he escaped to the carriage.

At home, chagrined over his social inadequacy, Frank reviewed the party step by step, picturing himself as suave and accomplished at conversational gambits. But it was months before he had the courage to try another party—this time with a different girl.

Frank felt cramped throughout his university career. The rules and regulations oppressed him; the competition baffled him. Where was architecture in all of this, he kept asking himself in the classroom. How could he get at inner meanings in architecture, in life itself? He liked surveying with a red and white field rod and testing materials, but his heart wasn't in engineering.

A senior at eighteen, Frank had a growing conviction that his great need was for experience in actual building. What good was a degree in engineering going to do him? Victor Hugo's prophecy burned in his mind and he longed to go to Chicago. Several of the country's finest architects had been attracted to that city. With great architects there, great architecture was inevitable, he reasoned. Surely if he went there he could find a job in some architect's office. And Uncle Jenkin Lloyd-Jones, minister at big, wealthy All Souls Church, would be at hand if he needed advice.

To continue to accept his mother's sacrifices for an education he didn't want wasn't good sense. But even when Frank explained his conflict to his mother she would not consent to his dropping out before graduation.

Casting about for a way to ease his mother's financial burden, he sold wooden novelties that he turned out on the scroll saw, but that was only a stopgap.

"At least write to Uncle Jenk," Frank begged his mother. After prolonged badgering, she did.

The letter that came back advised that Frank stay on at the University until he earned his degree. In Chicago, Uncle Jenk predicted, Frank would only waste his money on fine clothes and girls.

That Uncle Jenkin could so completely misunderstand Frank's avid desire to become an architect and also to aid his mother was maddening. It seemed useless to try to buck the resolute stubbornness of his mother and uncle. But Frank was as determined as they were: if he couldn't go with their consent, he'd go without it. It was now the late spring of 1887, and graduation was only a few weeks away, but Frank couldn't wait. The big problem was how to get enough money for train fare to Chicago.

Scouting around for possessions he might pawn, Frank assembled the fur collar of his overcoat, a prized copy of Plutarch's *Lives*, and a finely bound set of Gibbon's *Decline and Fall of the Roman Empire* for which he had scant respect. A pawnshop transaction netted funds for a ticket to Chicago with a surplus of seven dollars in cash.

A few days later Frank boarded a train for Chicago. He had left a note to his mother to account for an overnight absence. By the time she had become anxious about him, he thought, he'd have a job and could wire her his plans. He hated the subterfuge, but he had to begin his life work.

At 6:00 P.M. the train pulled into the Wells Street station in Chicago, where rain was falling in a slow drizzle. The faces of the crowd lighted by sputtering arc lights looked ghastly—tense and impersonal. Curiously Frank examined the arc lights, which he'd never seen before.

Since he had no particular destination he checked his baggage and set off on foot to find a place to spend the night. Disliking the thought of questioning a stranger about possible accommodations, he drifted along aimlessly, pausing on the Wells Street Bridge over the Chicago River to watch boats plying up and down the misty ribbon of water.

A bell clanged and people on the bridge began to run. Seeing that the bridge was about to swing out to let a grain boat through, Frank stood his ground so he could examine the hulk more closely. After the boat had gone through, drawn by a tug and belching clouds of steam, the bridge closed and Frank went on his way.

He stopped at a restaurant to eat dinner. When he came out again, it was raining in a more businesslike way and a damp chill penetrated to his bones. Attracted by a display of posters in front of the Chicago Opera House, he read, SIEBA, EXTRAVAGANZA BY GRAND CORPS DE BALLET.

A dollar was a lot to spend for it, but he would be warm and dry inside. During the hour he had to wait for the show to begin, his thoughts flew homeward. Would his departure increase the sadness in his mother's eyes?

The ballet carried Frank off into a world of dreams, although he liked the music better than the dancing, and after the show he couldn't resist riding a cable car—a new experience to him. Because the car was headed for the barn, his adventure was brief, but from there he took another car northward. The large numbers of ugly, glaring signs offended him. Finally, for what was left of the night, he took a room at Brigg's House. He felt alone, but not really lonely, for he was companioned by dreams of buildings he would design.

Full of hope he set off the next morning walking with long, eager steps. Where was the architecture of the great city, he asked himself. Along the dingy streets rows of buildings were lined up as if awaiting military inspection. Palmer House looked like a wrinkled old man. Frank had heard that American architects had borrowed from European ones, but he wasn't prepared for so prevalent a use of Romanesque—a style of architecture popular at the time of the Crusades. The massiveness, and the use of arcades, domes and elaborate ornamentation struck him as wrong for an industrialized, Midwestern city. Men no longer wore swords or armor; why should architecture be old-fashioned?

What distressed him even more was that many buildings were just a hash of imitative details borrowed from different styles of the past and then scrambled together. Too many stone fronts were false and fancy. Frank almost wished he could be less eye-conscious—and less ear conscious, too, he thought, acutely aware of the jangle, clop and clatter of vans, drays, and horses' hoofs. Steam, smoke, and the grayness of the sky made the whole city look dismal and a puffing Illinois Central train obstructed his view of the lake, where steamers were emitting rumbling whistles.

All day Frank tramped from office to office, drawing pitying, amused or scornful responses. After a twenty-cent supper at a bakery he returned to Brigg's House and asked to be moved to a seventy-five-cent room.

The second day was a repetition of the first except that Frank got his bag from the station and skipped meals, subsisting instead on ten cents' worth of bananas. That night he dreamed he was up in a balloon. His mother, holding frantically to a rope attached to the balloon, was being dragged along the ground. Although she called Jennie and Maginel to help her, the balloon escaped them and shot upward. Frank had the sensation of shooting up and up until he finally awoke. His mother could get along without him, he tried to reassure himself. She was self-reliant.

On the following morning Frank fared forth once more, but at the offices he visited he didn't get so much as a nibble. Consulting his dwindling list of possibilities he stood staring at the name Joseph Lyman Silsbee.

Silsbee, an outstanding architect, was at present working on Uncle Jenkin's All Souls Church. A word from Uncle Jenk would probably help, but Frank wanted to get a job by himself if possible. His feet ached from so much walking and he was hungry. He'd apply at Silsbee's, Frank decided, but he wouldn't disclose the fact that Jenkin Lloyd-Jones was his uncle.

The minute Frank stepped into Silsbee's office, he knew he'd like to work in a place like this. He admired Silsbee's sketches on the wall, and he liked the appearance of the bearded young man with a pompadour who came toward him with a friendly smile introducing himself as Cecil Corwin. Corwin had been humming a passage from *The Messiah*, and so, ignoring his primary purpose for being there, Frank asked, "Do you sing?"

"Try to," Corwin replied. After a brief conversation he asked to see some of Frank's drawings. "You've got a good touch," he remarked, and picking up the drawings he went off through a door marked *Private*.

Waiting for the verdict, Frank shifted impatiently in his chair. The situation was becoming critical. Unless he got a job—and soon—there wouldn't be money even for bananas.

4 *TOE IN THE DOOR*

FRANK LOOKED UP EXPECTANTLY WHEN THE DOOR TO SILSBEE'S private office opened. An aristocratic-looking, somber-faced man wearing eyeglasses with a long golden chain scrutinized him silently.

"Take him on as a tracer," Silsbee told Corwin. "Eight dollars a week." Without another word he retreated into his office.

Frank's work would be tracing designs, patterns, or drawings for blueprint reproduction. The salary didn't approach what he thought he was worth, but he had only twenty cents left in his pocket.

Cecil Corwin took him out to lunch and then, since it was Saturday and work would not resume until Monday, he insisted that Frank spend the weekend with him.

The Corwins were a congenial family and Frank enjoyed the dinner and evening of music. To ease his mind about his mother, he at last wrote her a letter, enclosing ten dollars borrowed from Cecil.

On Sunday Frank and Cecil set off to see how construction was coming on All Souls Church. "It's different," Cecil said before the building was in sight. "Not Gothic."

The Gothic style, characterized by pointed arches, high, narrow windows and tall, slim columns had been much copied by builders of American churches. However, All Souls Church, built of brick, with brown shingles, looked much more like a large residence or suburban clubhouse than a church. While Cecil investigated some details at close range, Frank strolled down Oakwood Boulevard to get an idea of how his uncle's church looked from a different angle. He was so absorbed in his study of it that he was startled when a firm hand gripped his shoulder and a voice boomed, "Well, young man, so here you are."

Frank whirled around to confront long-haired, bearded Uncle Jenkin, whose eyes were as compelling as in those days when he had preached in the chapel in the Valley.

Frank was remorseful when he heard that his mother, worried about him, had written Uncle Jenkin. As he was explaining that he'd sent her a letter, Cecil joined them and was astonished to discover that the two were related. Uncle Jenk insisted that Frank come and live with him.

Uncle Jenk's son, Dick, about Frank's own age, was keen, brilliant, ambitious, and witty. Aunt Susan was intellectual, but also very human, and although dynamic Uncle Jenk was sometimes opinionated, Frank found life at the parsonage interesting. Many leading citizens came to visit, Jane Addams of Hull House, and conductor Theodore Thomas among them.

Frank felt at ease about his mother after receiving a letter from her. She seemed reconciled to his decision and was pleased that he was with Uncle Jenkin. As usual she expressed anxiety about his clothes, diet, and morality, and advised him that if he should ever be confronted by a choice between success and Truth to choose Truth. "Keep close to the earth," she admonished.

Later, when Frank wanted to be on his own, Uncle Jenk found a room for him at the Watermans', only two blocks away from the parsonage. To move his possessions he and Dick used a wheelbarrow. The boarding house was decent and quiet, and Frank enjoyed the companionship of Harry Waterman, who was almost his age.

To keep in trim and also to save carfare, Frank frequently walked the forty blocks between Watermans' and the office. He liked his work as tracer and respected Mr. Silsbee, although he was aloof, impatient, and often almost contemptuous in the way he issued orders. Frank soon detected that Silsbee was more interested in drawing than in actual architectural procedures. This was not surprising, since Silsbee could easily turn out artistic, effective sketches, but Frank thought an architect owed his clients more than beautiful plans, and disapproved of Silsbee's slipshod methods of building.

Frank and Cecil, inseparable during the work day, also spent many evenings together attending Apollo Club programs and concerts conducted by Theodore Thomas. On Sundays Frank usually attended All Souls Church, where Uncle Jenkin preached with conviction and power to a large congregation, and afterwards Frank went to dinner at the parsonage.

At the end of three months at Silsbee's Frank's pay was raised to twelve dollars a week, and he had no reason for discontent until a new employee was taken on at eighteen dollars. When it became apparent that the new man was no more competent than he was, Frank seethed. He asked for a raise, received a flat no, and resigned.

He went to the firm of Beers, Clay, and Dutton because Clay had treated him considerately during his first job hunt, and after a brief discussion Clay offered him eighteen dollars a week. Frank was overjoyed. "I'm to start right in designing," he told Cecil jubilantly. Here was his chance to express his own ideas.

But he soon became acutely conscious that he wasn't equipped for the job. How could he produce designs when he didn't really know how to design? Failing to find anyone in the firm who could teach him, he informed Clay that he was leaving. Clay was astonished, but accepted the explanation of Frank's dilemma without rancor, whereupon Frank went immediately to Mr. Silsbee and asked to be reinstated.

After hearing the details Silsbee agreed to take him back at the same salary Clay had been paying him. It was good to be working with Cecil again. During their free time the two discussed everything from Gothic arches to love.

With Cecil, but also on solitary rambles, Frank constantly observed architectural patterns. One thing that puzzled him was the prevalence of top-heavy fakery like cornices. As far as he could see, these projecting decorative crowns served no good purpose— were, in fact, a deadly menace. In his mind's eye he could still picture the collapse of the capitol building in Madison when the dislodged cornice had teetered at a crazy angle, threatening the life of everyone who passed beneath it.

Although he was fascinated with architecture, Frank's life was not lopsided. He participated in study classes at All Souls Church and borrowed books from its circulating library. As a climax for their study of *Les Miserables*, Frank's class planned a supper with music and dancing at which students were to appear in costumes impersonating characters from the book. Frank was assigned the role of Enjolras, a young French officer, and arrived decked out in knee-length black boots, tight white trousers and scarlet military jacket adorned by epaulets, with a sword at his side.

The hall was gay with students costumed as Marat and other officials, and as peasant girls. Frank's sword kept getting in the way while he danced, but nothing could induce him to take it off. When it was time for refreshments, he was hurrying toward friends when he ran head on into a tall, pretty, teen-age girl with such momentum that she fell to her knees.

Although he was seeing stars, Frank managed to help her to her feet, and observed her fair skin and auburn curls approvingly. The girl, Catherine Tobin, laughed the incident off, but Frank could see a lump forming on her forehead.

Frank led her to where her parents were seated and his concern resulted in an invitation from the Tobins to come to dinner the next day.

Sunday morning, his interest in Victor Hugo stimulated by the study group, Frank went to the church library to borrow *Notre Dame*, which had so stirred him several years ago. This time he was challenged by the idea that there is a difference between romanticism and sentimentality. Walking to the Tobins' for dinner he mulled over what he had read.

In the Tobin house, everything seemed to center on Kitty, although she had three younger brothers. The atmosphere was one of gay informality and friendliness. After dinner Kitty suggested that she and Frank look at the new Kenwood houses in a fashionable residential district. With a tam-o'-shanter topping her curls Kitty, who was sixteen and a student in the Hyde Park High School, chattered about her activities, which included music lessons.

Things were going very well, Frank thought, as they walked briskly down the street. He had new friends and a job he liked, and the resources of Chicago at his disposal.

Although the city sometimes seemed crude and raw, it challenged him with a sense of big things to be done. His one anxiety was his mother. Her letters were brave, and with Jennie teaching country school her financial situation was improved; but Maginel was not yet very strong, and Frank surmised that his mother wanted to be with him, yet had too much pride to say so.

As soon as he could manage it, Frank wrote advising his mother to sell the Madison property and move to Chicago. Later, while he and Mrs. Wright were hunting a place not too close to the lake, because cold breezes would not be good for Maginel, Augusta Chapin, a Universalist pastor who was a friend of Frank's mother, invited the family to stay with her in Oak Park.

Going back and forth from his work Frank had plenty of opportunity to study the houses in the area. He disliked their jigsaw fretwork and curlicues, their cupolas and rambling front porches. To him turnip domes and scrollwork were unimaginative and meaningless. Frank couldn't see why anyone would build on midwest prairie land a gabled Queen-Anne-style house or one with battlemented towers under which no one would ever fight.

Bad houses bothered Frank because he felt people deserved beautiful places in which to live. Although Oak Park houses looked more like historical monuments than houses, he and the rest of the family liked the big shade trees and the quiet of the place and decided to make their home there. Jennie, Frank's sister, got a teaching job at the Chicago Avenue School.

For some time Frank had been dissatisfied with his work at Silsbee's. The gentle, well-bred architect was too conventional in his buildings to suit Frank, and he catered too much to the poor taste of some of his clients. On this subject Frank and Cecil disagreed. Cecil thought Silsbee should give his clients what they wanted, while Frank maintained that an architect should do the best he knew to elevate the standards of his clients. In the back of his mind Frank entertained the idea of making a change to another office.

One of the foremost firms was that of Burnham and Root, but despite some new ideas their work was mainly a patterning after Romanesque features. Another possibility was the office of Colonel William LeBaron Jenney, who had been General Sherman's Major of Engineering during the Civil War. In 1884–5 he had made news with the Home Insurance Building, a twelve-story structure in Chicago which was the first skeletal steel skyscraper in the world.

But rumor had it that Colonel Jenney was more of a *bon vivant* and gourmet than an architect. Frank's chief interest in him was that he had a share in training Louis Sullivan, considered the foremost rebel against old classical forms of architecture. Having thrown aside most of what he'd learned at the Beaux Arts in Paris, Sullivan had allied himself with engineer-architect Dankmar Adler. The innovations they were bringing to the construction of the Chicago Auditorium were exciting to everyone interested in building. But there wasn't an opening with Adler and Sullivan.

Frank had more on his mind than architecture. Ever since the *Les Miserables* party he had been visiting the Tobins frequently and taking Catherine to concerts. Distressed by Frank's seriousness, Cecil warned, "She's gay and charming, but she's only a child."

Even after Frank explained mutuality of interests was the main attraction, Cecil wouldn't let the matter drop, but urged Frank to go out with other girls. Mrs. Wright also voiced disapproval, pointing out the unsuitability of a high school girl's being singled out by a young man in business.

When Frank told Catherine about his mother's concern she admitted that schoolmates teased her and that her parents disapproved, but insisted she didn't care. However, a week later Frank had a note from Catherine saying that she'd been exiled to Mackinac for three months and was staying with relatives there.

With Catherine gone, Frank turned to work as an antidote, taking on extra projects. One of them was drawing plans for buildings at the Hillside Home School, located in the Valley and taught by his aunts Nell and Jane Lloyd-Jones.

But discontent with Silsbee's methods burgeoned. What Frank

was doing seemed artificial and false and he knew that his best
work could come only from within, from his heart.

One day Frank heard through another employee of Silsbee's
that there was an opening at the firm of Adler and Sullivan for a
draftsman who could help with the interior of the Chicago Auditorium.

Immediately Frank assembled drawings and struck off for the
firm's offices in the Borden Building. He hoped he'd get to see
Sullivan personally. Adler was the chief, the front man, but it was
his partner's ideas that interested Frank.

Sullivan, a handsome French-Irishman, had a dark, pointed
beard and was impeccably dressed. His big brown eyes looked
through and through Frank. After a question or two he unrolled
the sketches drawn somewhat in imitation of Silsbee's style.

Almost immediately Sullivan put them down. "No, no," he said
with a trace of irritation. "Draw something that is your own."

He'd rather work for Sullivan than any other architect in the
city, Frank told himself that night as he slaved away in his room
on freehand ornaments. Sullivan was the most advanced architect
in Chicago, possibly in the whole country. Striving to make his
drawings simple and clear, Frank persisted until three in the
morning. By Friday he had a dozen items ready for inspection.

In his office Sullivan was seated on a high stool at his drafting
board. With his nicotine-stained fingers he cast the drawings aside
one by one.

Frank watched the architect's face, seeking a sign of approval.
Sullivan studied one of the sketches while scratching his head with
a lead pencil, but made no comment. Instead he peeled the cover
sheet from his own drafting board. The excellence of the work
made Frank's seem amateurish by comparison and he could feel
his face flush with embarrassment.

Picking up a pencil Sullivan added a few strokes, then said
abruptly, "Wright, you have a good touch; you'll do. Can you
come Monday morning?"

He was in, Frank thought jubilantly. With Sullivan to guide
him, he was on the way to becoming the kind of architect he
wanted to be.

5 *T-SQUARE AND TRIANGLE*

DESPITE HIS CRITICISMS OF SILSBEE'S METHODS, FRANK HAD REALLY admired him, and it was with genuine regret that he left the firm this time. Having to say good-by to Cecil detracted from his pleasure in the new job.

"We can still meet for lunch and have evenings together," Cecil said wistfully.

But there'd no longer be the joy of sharing work. Frank wondered if changes leading to growth were always painful.

On Monday he reported to the office so early that only the energetic foreman, Paul Mueller, was on hand. Mueller was tall and ungainly, with a bristling black pompadour. Although young, he was already showing considerable promise as an architect. Somewhat officiously he assigned Frank a work space between two large windows on the south wall of the drafting room.

An office cub brought a drawing board and manila paper. As always, smooth untouched paper and an array of pencils made Frank itchy to be at work, but he had no assignment.

A short time later the other draftsmen trooped in noisily. After a few minutes of banter and witticisms, some at Frank's expense, they settled down to work. Feeling lonely among so many strangers, Frank occupied himself drawing on the margin of his stretch and sizing up the faces and attitudes of the other draftsmen.

About ten-thirty the door to Sullivan's office opened and Sullivan, holding a handkerchief to his nose, walked out with a pompous air that was almost a strut. "Ah, Wright, there you are," he said pleasantly, and handed him a sketch to be redrawn and inked in.

As Sullivan walked around checking the work of other draftsmen, Frank noticed that his dark eyes seemed to bore into persons and products alike. When in a loud, caustic voice he criticized a drawing of one of the workmen, the draftsman retorted hotly. Undoing the strings of his little black apron, he threw his pencil on his board, grabbed a leather case of drawing instruments, and stamped out.

Sullivan acted as if nothing had happened and continued his round of inspection, but Frank could feel the tension and surmised that incidents like this were not uncommon. He had some misgivings as to how long he could endure Sullivan's blasts.

Just before noon, senior partner Dankmar Adler came in. Frank knew his reputation as an engineer and constructor, but had never met the solidly built man who walked with a flat-footed gait. Passing among the tables he would pause occasionally and with a paternal attitude make a suggestion or exchange a greeting.

As he came toward Frank there was an expression of kindliness in his deep-set eyes under shaggy eyebrows. "Sullivan's new man?" he asked.

"Yes, sir," Frank replied.

Adler remarked that it was hard to give Sullivan exactly what he wanted; then, wishing Frank success, he made his way out of the office.

At first the office routine seemed strange and unfriendly—and Sullivan, whose standards were unremittingly high, was very critical.

"Bring it alive," Sullivan kept admonishing Frank as he inspected his assignments in connection with the Chicago Auditorium. Picking up a pencil, he would with a few deft strokes inject an almost poetic quality.

Many times a day Sullivan would summon Frank with the imperious call of "Wright! Wright!"

Learning not so much through what Sullivan taught as through observation Frank began to use the T-square and triangle in a way that brought him new joy in his work. Although Frank disliked Sullivan's smoking, swearing, and drinking, he admired his free and independent spirit, his sense of drama, his beautiful language of self-expression.

From the standpoint of his own work, Frank was glad he'd made the change to the office of Adler and Sullivan. The big drawback was lack of companionship. Frank's heavy, rather long hair was the object of raillery. The office gang, resenting his individuality and arty tastes, symbolized in the wearing of a flowing tie, subjected him to horseplay. Sullivan's approval of Frank and his work in contrast with his haughty scorn for the other draftsmen widened the gap.

When two of the office gang invited him to join them in boxing during the noon hour in a back room where some of the employees ate lunch, Frank knew they hoped to pit him against the pugilistic Bill Gaylord, who would give him a drubbing.

Frank was confident that he had the stamina to take Gaylord on, but although he had boxed for fun, he had never been briefed on the science of boxing; so he stalled for time. Meanwhile he went to a fencing and boxing academy and asked for some rough training. In the space of two weeks he crowded in twelve lessons. How much help they would be, Frank wasn't sure, since his teacher was more of a fencer than a boxer. But he was ready to take on any comers.

One morning Frank turned to Isbell, a bugle-voiced, conceited blond, and inquired, "Boxing this noon?"

Isbell nodded. "Come along and put on the gloves," he urged.

Seeing knowing winks exchanged among the draftsmen, Frank pretended to be hesitant. In the back room he took off his coat, vest, and collar, and put on the dirty boxing gloves Bill Gaylord offered him.

His first challenger was the jaunty Isbell, familiarly known as Izzy. Obviously strong, he turned out to be a slugger. Although Frank got a cut on the lip, the boxing lessons enabled him to outmaneuver Izzy. When he banged Izzy hard on the nose, Gaylord, a friend of Izzy's called, "Time!"

Maintaining he'd understood that this was to be a one-round contest, Frank continued the punishing blows. Frank saw surprise on the faces of the gang, but got no applause for his strategy.

"Here, Izzy, it's my turn," Gaylord finally insisted.

Gaylord, who had won honors as a boxer, was awkward but sturdy. It was evident that he was enraged by the pummeling Izzy had received. Craftily he rocked and crouched in perpetual motion. Up to now Frank had rather liked Gaylord, but his attitude at this moment aroused Frank to furious action. Combining speed with strength, Frank toppled him, but Gaylord claimed he'd done it on fouls.

At that Frank lost his temper and tore into Gaylord verbally, challenging him to fight bare-handed. The gang intervened, suggesting that the match be fixed for some other time.

Frank knew how the gang would "fix" it and said so, pointing out their unsportsmanlike procedure of pitting two boxers against him in one round. Throwing down his gloves, he walked out. Regrets mingled with his anger. It had been his hope that by making a good showing as a boxer he could silence the taunts about his artiness. If he'd taken on his two challengers good-humoredly, he'd have won backers. Now every man in the office would be his enemy.

His forebodings were well founded. Ottie, ringleader of the office gang, became increasingly insolent. But the insinuations and bedevilment were less hard to bear when Sullivan let Frank bring in George Elmslie as his assistant and understudy. Frank had known the young draftsman at Silsbee's. A Scotsman, George was slow of speech and movement, but a conscientious worker. Although quiet and somewhat timid, he was very loyal to Frank.

One noon hour Frank and George had stayed after all the other draftsmen except Ottie had left for lunch. Ottie topped off a series of insults with, "You're just a Sullivan toady, Wright."

On other occasions his coworker had said more insulting things than this, but today Frank's patience was overtaxed. Laying down his pencil he looked at the self-satisfied Ottie and decided he'd taken all he was going to take. Frank walked over to him and knocked him to the floor. Jumping up, Ottie grabbed a knife and advanced with murderous intent. Slashed several times, Frank seized a maple T-square and swung it, catching Ottie's neck just above the collar. Ottie dropped the knife and sank to the floor.

"I'll pay you for this," he told Frank as he got to his feet, and weaving a little, went to his desk, took his instruments, and left.

"Call Cecil," Frank directed George, realizing that his wounds were numerous.

Cecil, only five blocks away, came immediately and took Frank to the office of his brother, who was a physician.

That evening Frank went to see Catherine, who had returned recently from the North. The separation had not changed their devotion, but Kitty was thinner, paler, less gay.

As the weeks passed, Frank and Kitty realized that parent-monitored conversations and occasional musical programs weren't going to satisfy them, but matrimony posed too big a financial problem. Things got to the point where they felt they could no longer put up with the barrages of criticism. Unless they found freedom soon, the relationship would be ruined, thought Frank, but he was at a loss to know what to do.

Meanwhile, conditions improved at the office. After Ottie's departure for the Beaux Arts in Paris, hostility waned. Sullivan, who lived alone, was now relying on Frank, whom he always called Wright, for advice and companionship. Although only in his mid-thirties, he seemed older to Frank, then nineteen. Sullivan would for hours on end discuss his architectural philosophy, in which he was far ahead of his time. A champion of independence, he frowned on imitations and saw no sense in schoolhouses with Greek columns or theatres with Moorish domes.

Sullivan had scant respect for most architects, although he admired the dignity and originality of Henry Hobson Richardson, who had died in 1886. Basically adventurous, Richardson, the architect for Trinity Church in Boston, had moved in the direction of seeking to create buildings expressing the age. But Sullivan deplored the fact that instead of emerging with a new style for an industrial age, he had let clients tie him down to the Romanesque style to which he had merely added innovations—rich texture, colorful interiors, and spaciousness—thereby popularizing a style that was basically an imitation.

Architects, Sullivan believed, should abandon monumental forms of the past and create forms that would meet the needs of the present with a maximum of space, light, freedom, and beauty.

Frank and Sullivan did not always confine their conversation to building. Mutually interested in books, philosophy, and music, they talked about everything from Beethoven symphonies to Walt Whitman's *Leaves of Grass*. Encouraged by Sullivan's friendliness, Frank one day confided to him that he wanted to marry but had the double handicap of parental objections and financial difficulties. After hearing a little about Catherine, Sullivan called Adler and proposed they give Frank a five-year contract.

Adler agreed, leaving details up to Sullivan. An idea flashed into Frank's mind. If he was to be with the firm for five years, why not ask for a loan for enough money to finance building a home? Each month he could pay back a little out of his salary.

In response to his proposal Sullivan not only lent him money of his own, but also went with him to Oak Park to see the rolling, wooded lot on Forest Avenue that Frank wanted to buy. Elated by Sullivan's approval, Frank made plans for marriage.

6 *BETRAYED BY FINE PRINT*

FRANK WENT AHEAD ENERGETICALLY WITH PLANS FOR HIS OWN house in Oak Park, but pressures of work left little time for personal projects. Before the Chicago Auditorium was open for public use, Adler and Sullivan moved to new offices in the tower rising majestically above it. Paul Mueller continued to be Adler's right-hand man, while Frank was Sullivan's. At his side in his own glassed-in cubicle Frank had the faithful, cooperative George Elmslie. Their windows afforded a view of Lake Michigan. One of the doors in the cubicle led into the drafting room, where thirty draftsmen of all ages were employed; another led into Sullivan's office.

Among the tasks Sullivan apportioned Frank was the selection of names of great musicians to be cast in high relief on both sides of the huge proscenium arch in the auditorium. Frank's choices, ranging from Berlioz to Wagner, went unchallenged.

Working with him, Sullivan had much to say about simplicity, about ornamentation which would be *of* the thing and not on it as a mere applied surface decoration. Sullivan gave practical force to his statements in the way he designed the lighting for the auditorium. Hitherto devices for illumination had been something added, usually in the form of chandeliers. In the auditorium lights were recessed in artistic ornament as an integral part of the interior.

Introspective and egocentric Sullivan frequently relieved his loneliness and restlessness by talking hours on end to Frank—

often after office hours. While Sullivan, his eyes flashing with enthusiasm, discoursed on architecture, poetry, or democracy, Frank would sit listening for the most part, occasionally glancing out at the lighted city and the Bessemer steel converters reddening the night sky. Often Sullivan continued until Frank would have to take the last suburban train, which brought him into Oak Park at a late hour.

Frank's architectural philosophy during this period was being shaped not only by Sullivan but by the writings of other architects. One of these was Viollet le Duc, who when head of the École des Beaux Arts had said, "My chief object is truth."

Sullivan, also an uncompromising searcher after principle, fostered Frank's hunger for integrity, pointing out how buildings that wallowed in turrets, pinnacles, gables, and arches in passive imitation of styles of the past were architectural lies. "In Chicago," he said, "there is a different civilization on every corner."

More clearly than ever Frank saw that each artist's technique must be his own. But philosophy was sidetracked as the date for dedication of the auditorium drew near. Erected at a cost of three million dollars, the building also included a hotel and offices. The auditorium proper seated six thousand people and incorporated revolutionary improvements.

Prior to this, Adler, with a knowledge of acoustics unique in his generation, had invented the sounding board—a sloping surface extending above the proscenium and extending into the audience room. In the auditorium, Sullivan had developed the sounding board so that it magnified and projected the sound. All opposing wall surfaces to the rear were deadened by lime mortar an inch thick, which made the acoustics excellent.

A kind of air conditioning was provided by warm air pouring out through perforations on the face of the arches. Adler was a splendid builder and farsighted planner, thought Frank, inspecting the auditorium when it was finished, but Sullivan had made it sing.

The opening on December ninth was a gala event. Governor Fifer was there, as well as Chicago's élite. After addresses and felicitations Benjamin Harrison, President of the United States, spoke briefly. Operatic star Adelina Patti sang "Home Sweet Home." Local papers ran off whole editions honoring the event.

Ferdinand Peck, prime promoter of the auditorium, wanted the President's words of praise carved on a tablet to be put in the foyer. The designing of it was left to Wright.

Although skyrocketed to fame, Adler seemed more sober than elated. Sullivan was cocky but exhausted, and went to Ocean Springs, Mississippi, to rest. In his absence Frank became better acquainted with Adler. He had always admired Adler's skill and inexorable honesty, but now he saw a new side to him—his generosity and salty wisdom.

Into the office poured commissions for office buildings, factories, hotels and theaters. Back from his vacation Sullivan shared plans for several new buildings. One day, walking with a firm, springy tread, he came into Frank's cubicle and put a drawing board down on his table. On the manila paper stretch he had drawn a delicately penciled elevation.

"I've never seen anything like it," Frank exclaimed in honest admiration. Colonel Jenney's skeletal steel Home Insurance Building had upset the custom of supporting buildings by means of a solid mass of masonry, but it looked like a glass-enclosed cage perched on two stories of solid granite—and it had cornices and other traditional features.

Sullivan's sketch was clearer and sharper than the Home Insurance Building. It had structural vigor. Although it was tall, it didn't look like a tower stacked on something else.

"Wainwright Building for St. Louis," Sullivan said proudly.

In discussing it he had much to say about form following function. Buildings, he told Frank, were of no significance unless they reflected the needs of the people using them. American sculptor Horatio Greenough and earlier architects had set forth the "form-follows-function" idea, but Sullivan elaborated on it.

During out-of-office hours Frank and Catherine were busy with plans for their marriage. He was now barely twenty, she not yet eighteen. The wedding in the early summer of 1890 was not a cheerful occasion. While Uncle Jenkin performed the ceremony to the accompaniment of parental tears, a dreary rain poured down outside. For their honeymoon the couple went off to the Valley.

A few weeks later they returned to Chicago. On the way across town on foot to the house that was being built for them in Oak

Park, Frank and Catherine had their first quarrel. He wanted to carve mottoes in the panels of the doors of their home. Catherine objected.

The house had a steep, pyramid-shaped roof with hovering eaves and windows that met and turned corners. Bare-faced compared with its neighbors, the dwelling had stark but compelling lines. Screened porches overlooked a terraced lawn. Inside there weren't any mottoes on the doors, but carved over the fireplace in the living room was "Truth is life."

Catherine was an interesting companion, but Frank was not so immersed in his new home life as to be unaware of the architectural experiments going on in Chicago. The most formidable rival of Adler and Sullivan in making the Chicago skyline impressive was the firm of Daniel H. Burnham and John Wellborn Root. To their credit Burnham and Root had functional, solid buildings featuring firsts in fireproofing and floating foundations—broad rafts of concrete reinforced by iron rails. Root, a civil engineer, had a great flair for invention.

The new twenty-one story Masonic Temple designed by Burnham and Root was then the tallest structure in the world. It had many good qualities, Wright thought, but form and function had not been so skillfully wedded as in Sullivan's Wainwright Building.

Thinking about form and function led Frank on to the subject of nature—not the out-of-doors or animal life, but the inner reality of things. This idea extended to the use of material. The nature of brick was its brickness, and of wood, its woodness. Why try to make materials look like something they weren't?

At Silsbee's Frank had learned much about house planning, but Adler and Sullivan refused to build residences. When important clients insisted on dwellings, the designs were assigned to Frank to work on outside office hours. These were checked on by the firm, but there was little interference.

The extra income was welcome when within the year a son named Lloyd was born. Catherine was no more sensible about finances than Wright himself, who carried paper money crumpled in his pockets, never knowing at any given moment what his assets were.

Frank liked to design houses, and liked the added independence. At times he was tempted to leave the firm, but he felt he owed too much to Sullivan to walk out on him. Besides, he was still under contract. Sometimes Frank wondered if Sullivan wasn't more interested in philosophy than in his newest project, which would embody the most advanced architectural practices of the day.

It was clear to Frank that the skyscraper was not the product of any one man. This type of building had come about naturally in response to rising land values, development of structural steel, floating foundations and the electric elevator, still in an experimental stage. But Sullivan was giving skyscrapers beauty.

A favorite subject for conversation in the early months of 1891 was the Columbian Exposition to be held in Chicago in 1893, scheduled to bring together artistic and architectural talent from all over America. Burnham was to be chief of construction, Root consulting architect.

At first both Wright and Sullivan were excited, seeing in the Fair an opportunity to advance a truly American architecture. But before plans were complete in 1891, Root died at the age of forty-three, and Burnham, who had a sense of inferiority about Midwest culture, let the Easterners in the Commission of Architects dominate. The result was a decree that all buildings at the Fair should be classical in style. This meant a throwback to Greek usages—Doric, Ionic, and Corinthian columns, cornices, friezes, scrolls and acanthus leaves.

When approached to build the Transportation Building, Sullivan assented, but declared that it would look like what it was, a house for locomotives, and not be patterned after a Greek temple or a Roman bath.

Meanwhile Wright was faced with mounting debts incurred through extravagant habits, payments on his house, and the birth of a second son, John. It seemed feasible to accept some work on his own initiative and time. Since clients served through the firm had been satisfied with the residences he had built for them, it was not hard to work up business on his own. The commissions enabled Wright to make final payment on the Oak Park house.

Gleefully he went into Sullivan's office to ask for the deed, but

Sullivan adopted a haughty, imperious attitude and refused to give it to him on the grounds that Wright had broken the contract.

"How?" asked Wright in an aggrieved tone.

"Read your contract."

While Wright was examining the contract Sullivan went on to say that he knew about the house he was building for Dr. Harlan and that the contract had forbidden work outside office hours.

With a sinking heart Frank saw in the hitherto unread fine print that what Sullivan said was true. But it seemed unjust. If he could work overtime for the firm, why couldn't he do it for himself?

"Taking outside commissions hasn't made me inefficient on my job, has it?" he challenged Sullivan.

Sullivan admitted that it hadn't, but said he wanted no division of efforts. Pointing out that initial contacts with clients had come through the firm, he succeeded in conveying the idea that Wright was immature and dishonest. The way Sullivan put it made him wonder if he'd stolen the Harlan house contract from the firm.

He probably owed Sullivan an apology, thought Wright, but at the same time he wanted to justify his actions. When Sullivan adamantly refused to give him the deed, Wright left his office with the intention never to return.

Several days later Adler mailed him the deed. Now that his anger had cooled, he wanted to see Sullivan again, not to resume work, but to square himself. Swallowing resentment and chagrin he went to the office. He was deeply hurt and surprised when Sullivan said, "Wright, your conduct has been so perfidious there is nothing I care to hear you say."

He'd taken too much for granted, Wright admitted as he left Sullivan's office, but he hadn't been perfidious. Dejected and humiliated, he didn't know what step to take next. He did not want to lose the friendship of a man he had respected and admired, but Sullivan had closed the door on any possibility of reconciliation.

7
DESIGNER OF HOUSES, A PLAYROOM, AND A WINDMILL

CUT OFF FROM LOUIS SULLIVAN, WRIGHT DECIDED TO GO INTO business on his own and persuaded his friend Cecil Corwin to take offices with him on a floor in the tower of the Schiller Building. No partnership existed except in the sharing of facilities. Each had a private drafting room, but they used jointly an anteroom and a business office furnished with a seven-foot-square table, chests of drawers, and chairs. Indian statuettes and glass-diffused artificial light gave the waiting room an air of elegance. Pridefully Frank studied the plate-glass door with his and Cecil's name in gold letters. Full of enthusiasm over their plans for the future, the two friends visualized the clients that would soon be streaming through the doors.

Because of his experience in connection with the designing of theaters for Adler and Sullivan, Wright had expected to be called upon for similar projects, but he wasn't. As a matter of fact, he was more interested in building houses than public buildings. There was no precedent for the kind of houses he wanted to build, but he knew what he liked and disliked.

He wouldn't put up bedeviled boxes like the ones in Oak Park— houses cut full of holes to let in air and light. Nor would his residences be overdressed with rosettes, fan tails and jiggerwork. Gables, minarets, bay windows and fancy porches he regarded as nonsensical affectations. He meant to eliminate attics and basements, which were damp, dark, musty catchalls.

Wright's first client in the office at the Schiller Building was

W. H. Winslow of the Winslow Ornamental Iron Works, who wanted a house at River Forest. Something of an architect himself, he appreciated what Wright was trying to do.

In building the Winslow house Wright utilized horizontal lines. Each wing—each room, in fact—extended into a garden. A low, projecting roof emphasized the sense of shelter. Beneath the overhanging eaves there was a terra cotta frieze. Personal and distinctive, the house became an attraction. Some who saw it admired it, but many ridiculed it because it went counter to the architectural patterns endorsed by the much-publicized Columbian Exposition.

Visitors to the fair were enthralled by the white wooden buildings in their enforced uniformity of cornice, color, and style. Fluttering banners, fountains, lagoons, emerald lawns and the shimmering water of Lake Michigan just beyond the grounds gave the impression of a dream world.

But when Wright passed through the turnstile, the buildings struck him as an artistic calamity. Scrolls and columns had been appropriate in the ancient world, but they seemed alien and snobbish for an industrialized, urban country. America had been founded on the principle of freedom; her architecture should be free too. Everything was fraudulent except Sullivan's Transportation Building. That looked like what it was—a shed for trains; but on the long walls imaginative use had been made of polychrome decorations. Because the building was neither Romanesque nor classic, Fair authorities regarded it as a black sheep. But Wright was delighted when Sullivan was commended by the Paris Beaux Arts for his originality and presented with a gold medal.

Wright enjoyed the cultural aspects of the fair more than the architecture. In the Ho-o-den, a half-scale wooden replica of a temple, he saw exhibits of Japanese art. Through books and acquaintance with his former employer Silsbee, he had acquired some knowledge of Oriental craftsmanship, but now he was captivated by the simplicity of line and details in the woodcuts of Hokusai and Hiroshige.

The only effect the fair had on Wright was to strengthen his resolution not to dress his houses in frills borrowed from other times and other lands. One of the admirers of his techniques was

Edward C. Waller. At a dinner in the Waller home, which Frank and Catherine Wright attended, other guests were the handsome, dignified Daniel H. Burnham and his wife. Uncle Dan, as Waller called the tall, athletic architect, had a magnetic personality.

After dinner, while the women talked, Mr. Waller took the men into the library. Young Wright was stunned when Mr. Burnham came forth with a magnanimous offer to give him financial backing for four years of study at the Beaux Arts in Paris, plus two years in Rome with a job waiting for him when he got back home.

The generosity of the offer, which included provisions for Wright's family, was overwhelming, but he didn't want what the Beaux Arts had to offer. From Sullivan, who had studied there, he had acquired a distrust for the school's traditional, hidebound techniques. But how could he make an appropriate explanation for his refusal?

"Another year and it will be too late," Mr. Burnham pulled at one end of his heavy mustache.

"It's too late now," Wright blurted forth. Haltingly he tried to make clear the urgency he felt about developing his own style.

Mr. Burnham, whose square chin gave evidence of determination, pointed out that the fair would have a tremendous influence on architecture. The trend, he said, would be toward classical buildings, and architects trained in the classical techniques would be much in demand.

As the arguments went on and on, Frank had the sensation of being trapped.

"Think of your future; think of your family," urged Mr. Waller, who had been pacing around restlessly.

Frank fidgeted uncomfortably. The plan just outlined would be safe and easy. Study abroad would be interesting, and in Burnham's reputable firm he'd be assured both prestige and financial security. But to take this course would mean a surrender of his individuality, of his beliefs about architecture. And was he willing to exchange the excitement of pioneering for the dullness of security? Both by inheritance and training he was a rebel.

"Well?" asked Burnham with a kindly smile.

If he abandoned his own ideals just to gain financial success he'd never be on good terms with himself, thought Frank. He'd rather give his loyalty to what he believed in, even if he failed. "I'm grateful," he said, getting to his feet, "but I can't accept the offer."

As they left the library, Frank knew they must be thinking he was stubborn, perverse, and a little crazy, but he couldn't help it.

When Frank fell behind on rent for the Schiller office he almost regretted his decision. The birth of the third child, named Catherine after her mother, was an occasion for happiness, but increased the already worrisome financial obligations. Sometimes there wasn't even money for groceries.

So Wright was pleased when the Moores, neighbors on Forest Avenue, came to confer with him about a new home. Deflation set in when Mr. Moore said he wanted something less radical than the Winslow house. Unable to out-argue lawyer Moore, Wright wanted to reject the commission, but his children needed shoes, so he gave in, building a more conventional house that made the Moores happy but left him dissatisfied. No more compromises, he vowed.

Other commissions followed, and Wright was so busy that he saw little of Cecil Corwin. That troubled him, because his friend was looking more and more discouraged. One day Cecil confessed that he was finding no joy in his work and meant to give up his office and go east.

Wright reproached, pleaded, cajoled, but could not dissuade him. "I don't want to go on seeing you do things I can't," he said.

"Why not join me, Cecil?"

Cecil shook his head. "I'm not the kind of partner you need." Walking over to Wright he put a hand on his shoulder. "You are going to go far. Not everybody would pay the price in hard work and sacrifice that you'll make for it."

Now that his decision had been made, Cecil looked happy again; but Frank couldn't shake off the sense of loss, although he now had numerous colleagues and other friends. Because of his dynamic convictions and his natural leadership a clique of young architects, converts to the new architecture—Dwight Perkins, Myron Hunt, Bob Spencer and others—had formed around him.

There was also a luncheon club of like-minded architects calling themselves "The Eighteen." Most of them admired what Wright was doing, but were timid and cautious about developing revolutionary techniques for their own building.

Disciples and friends didn't fill the void Cecil had left and the office seemed lonely. When Dwight Perkins mentioned that his loft in the Steinway Building was too big for him, Frank and several of the young architects of "The Eighteen" moved in. The group shared a waiting room staffed by a receptionist and stenographer. In the big attic overhead they had a private studio-like drafting room.

Business was not exactly brisk. Daniel Burnham had been right about the influence the 1893 fair would exert. Crowds had been impressed by the buildings, not realizing that the real beauty had lain in the unity of the architecture, not in the style. They returned home demanding columns, scrolls and pediments, whether suitable or not. The American Institute of Architects fostered the trend by providing architects who could build in classical style.

Occasionally the Steinway Hall architects went out to speak to clubs. At Hull House Wright read a paper on "The Art and Craft of the Machine" before the Arts and Crafts Society, then in the process of organization. In it he proclaimed the importance and inevitability of the machine. For a time Wright too had been alarmed at the shoddiness and conformity of machine-made products, but now he had come to the conclusion that architects and artists should not shun the essential tools of the industrial age. They should, however, dominate the machine instead of letting the machine dominate them.

Most of the artists, architects and professors present thought Wright's ideas extreme and argued that the machine was antagonistic to art. He agreed that antiques or Oriental rugs turned out by mechanical processes would be meaningless; but used as a creature and not a creator, the machine would serve well.

Next day there was an editorial in the *Chicago Tribune* commenting on the fact that an artist had spoken in defense of the machine as a tool.

Up to now Wright's work had shown the influence of Sullivan, but a streamlined house built for Ward Willets in Highland Park gave proof that he was on his own. In his spare time he designed for his children a large, barrel-ceiling playroom with fanciful chandeliers and a scene from *The Arabian Nights* over the fireplace.

While working on this, Wright kept dreaming of an adequate studio at home where he could have easy, constant access to his work; and a contract with Luxfer Prism Company to act as consulting engineer for making glass installations in a number of office buildings made this improvement possible.

A gigantic old willow tree between the studio and the house posed a problem until Frank conceived the idea of enclosing the tree in the passageway connecting the two buildings. The roof, like a collar around it, was watertight, but permitted the willow to grow.

Frank's layout included a study, library, reception room and drafting room which he built on his own except for help from friends, including George Elmslie. The skylighted studio was decorated with statues and flowers, and with Japanese prints which inspired Wright with their economy of line. Soon he had several draftsmen and a secretary, Isabel Roberts, working for him.

To have his studio at hand where he could create far into the night was a great joy, but there were also drawbacks. Now family crises intruded on his working hours. Even with his mother and Catherine's mother on hand frequently to help with the children, quarrels and squabbles arose that were audible in the studio. Sometimes when consulting a client Wright would notice a door being opened stealthily, then one or more curly-haired children would peer around curiously.

In 1896 Frank's maiden aunts Nell and Jane wanted a windmill erected over the reservoir for their country boarding school known as the Hillside Home School, located in the Valley. Could they have an artistic one instead of an ugly steel tower, they wanted to know. Frank designed a hexagonal wooden tower sixty feet high to sheath the framework. Although he planned for it to set solidly

Willets House, Highland Park, Illinois

on a rock foundation, the Lloyd-Jones uncles and the contractor
vetoed it. It would come crashing down in the first windstorm,
they declared. Why not get the usual kind of windmill—practical
and cheap.

But the aunts, who had vigor and independence, asked Frank to
go ahead. Once while the tower was in process of construction he
went to check on it. Timothy, a Welsh stonemason and family
friend, had made the stone foundation even sturdier than the
plans called for. Frank was satisfied that unless torn up by the
roots the tower could not fall.

The aunts dubbed the windmill Romeo and Juliet—Romeo the
working part, Juliet the ornamental. At sight of the finished tower
standing staunch yet graceful like a sentinel overlooking the
Valley, Frank was well pleased.

Back at the studio in Oak Park he was confronted by the fact
that although he was earning good commissions there never
seemed to be money enough to go around. Both Frank and
Catherine were haphazard in their business dealings, writing
checks at random until informed they had depleted their fund in
the bank.

Frank loved fine books and prints; he wanted his children to
have access to what was beautiful in music and art; and he wanted
the best clothes available for his children and for Catherine, who
dressed smartly. The birth of another child, David, added to the
expenses.

When the grocer presented Frank with a sheaf of long-overdue
bills, he was remorseful and taken aback. He'd have to economize
until he found a way to earn more money.

8 *VOLUNTARY EXILE*

IN TRYING TO ECONOMIZE, WRIGHT FOUND IT EASIER TO DO WITHOUT the so-called necessities than the luxuries. Temptations to live beyond his means were always coming his way. In 1897 he became involved in a printing project with former client W. H. Winslow. Together they turned out a limited number of copies of *The House Beautiful*. Small folios half calf with gilt top were printed by hand by Auvergne Press on handmade paper. Frank did not sell the copies, but gave them away to friends.

An increase in the number of clients eased the financial situation, but frequently those who came wanted a Colonial house, a Cape Cod cottage, or the multi-storied, gingerbread type then popular. Frank, who resented borrowed styles for houses as much as for public buildings, would offer highly original counter proposals.

Because he loved the prairies he wanted the houses he built on them to have a unity with rocks, streams and trees. Clients were amenable when he talked about relating a structure to its site, but were usually exasperated when he insisted on low-slung, earth-hugging houses with horizontal lines that meant elimination of a basement or attic. And some were dubious about the necessity for fireplaces or recessed illumination. Electric lights were still not common and certain clients wanted to advertise their presence with showy chandeliers.

Occasionally Wright's healthy ego or uncompromising vigor repelled a would-be client, but many were won by his sincerity and zest. Despite his efforts to convert clients to pet ideas, he did have a concern for their needs. His goal was to build not houses that were mere shelters, but houses that would add to the security and happiness of those who lived in them.

By 1903 Wright was building widely in Chicago. His residences, often referred to as Prairie Houses, got that name because of his insistence that the prairie called for a different type of dwelling. In Springfield, Illinois, he built one of these for Mrs. Susan L. Dana, who needed a place to display her art collection and also entertain extensively. Roughly the shape of a letter T, the house had dignity and fine proportion and became a showplace.

Because Wright's houses looked different and violated traditional architectural principles, he incurred the ridicule of conservatives. Bankers refused to finance the "queer houses." Millmen would hand his plans back saying they'd only be inviting trouble if they filled his order. Puzzled contractors sometimes failed to read his blueprints correctly. In headlong pursuit of his architectural ideals, Wright remained staunch and persistent in the face of hostile criticism and obstacles. Unfortunately the audacity of his outspoken defense incurred the enmity of some architects and prospective clients who really admired his brilliance and integrity.

Building prairie houses and an oak and sandstone structure for his aunts' Hillside Home School increased Wright's income, but his expenses had also spiralled. The birth of Llewellyn in 1903 brought the number of his children up to six, a daughter Frances having been born five years earlier. The Wright home had become a lively place. When Frank brought in balloons by the dozen the house resembled a carnival. His laughter was as exuberant as that of the children.

Holidays were gala occasions. At Christmastime socks dangled from the fireplace mantel in the playroom. One Christmas Wright gave bicycles to all the children old enough to ride them. On another each received a musical instrument.

Wright was not very adroit at disciplining his high-spirited, self-willed children. Once when supposedly buying a suit for John at Marshall Field's he also purchased him a three-foot-long Franco-Prussian sword because John staged a tantrum.

Playing the role of father often baffled Wright, but he did try to give the children values and a sense of belonging. As a family they did a lot of reading together—especially when Grandmother Wright was there.

Among the houses built in 1904, his greatest satisfaction came in designing a cream-white brick one for Robert M. Lamp of Madison—Robie of school days. Modest in size and materials, the house had a quaint roof garden.

A challenge of a different nature presented itself when Wright got a commission from the Larkin Company in Buffalo, New York, to design a factory building. Here was his chance, he thought gleefully, to make a protest in brick and mortar against the spread of classical architecture that had been responsible for making banks, libraries, and schools look as if they'd been transplanted from Greece or Rome.

In his planning Frank was dominated by the idea that the form must be determined by the function. He gave much attention to features that would contribute to the comfort and safety of the workers. The model he came up with was a steel-structured cliff of brick which he planned to have hermetically sealed to keep the interior free from smoke.

After the contract had been let to Paul Mueller, who since the dissolution of Adler and Sullivan in 1895 had been on his own, Wright had another idea. Why not build stair towers free of the central block? They would be a means of communication and escape, but also would serve as air intakes for the ventilating system. To convince Larkin that the stairways were worth an added expenditure of thirty thousand dollars, Frank took the train to Buffalo for a personal interview. Larkin consented.

The completed building had beauty and dignity, with exterior ornamentation accomplished through skillfully placed accents of sculpture. Its metal-bound plate-glass doors were an architectural novelty. The interior of the building was really one large room with five stories of galleries opening on a central court. Vitreous, cream-colored brick and ample lighting made the working quarters attractive and cheerful.

On the top story were a restaurant and a conservatory with flowers and ferns. Paved with brick, the roof served as a recreation area. With Wright-designed furniture of steel and magnesite, a new material, the building was completely fireproof. At a time when air conditioning was in its infancy this structure breathed through vast ducts at the corners. Employees were pleased with their new quarters. Although the Larkin family found the building a little too severe, its clean lines, solidity, and sheer surfaces were prophetic of architecture to come.

Wright was beginning to have the reputation of one who built well, if daringly. Already imitators had begun to copy some of his innovations like his practice of bringing ceilings down to fit the height of ordinary individuals. But those who borrowed without understanding the principles involved cheapened their products.

The *Architectural Record* of July, 1905 commended Wright's work, calling attention to the truthful relationship between structure and design, the frank expression of the quality of material, the absence of artificial ornament.

From the Larkin Building Wright turned to plans for Unity Temple to be erected in Oak Park. In it he wanted to test some of his new ideas concerning space. Interiors of cathedrals had been hollowed out of sculptured masses. But instead of determining the inside according to the outside, why not let space within shape the edifice?

For the Unity Temple the prime necessity was a room for worship. Let that shape the building. Working on the plans nights because they were freest from interruptions, Frank would remind himself to keep the lines clear, to strive for harmony and proportion. Sometimes encouraged by strains from Catherine's playing of Bach or Beethoven, he would stay at his drawing board until dawn. For Unity Temple, which included a separate building for educational and recreational activities, Wright made and rejected thirty-five plans.

Handicapped by the necessity for using a cheap building material—the church had only forty-five thousand dollars to spend—he hit upon the idea of a monolith constructed of concrete cubes. When Dr. Johonnot, Universalist pastor of Unity Temple, saw the plans, he exclaimed, "No spire?" in a tone of shocked disapproval.

Unity Temple, Oak Park, Illinois

Studying types of architecture Wright too had felt some admiration for the upward thrust of the great cathedrals, but a spire was only a symbol. Couldn't aspiration be expressed in some other way? Before Wright had won Dr. Johonnot's support, other members of the board began objecting to the cubical interior with four equal arms. Because the Unity Temple site was exposed to heavy traffic, the plan called for an auditorium enclosed on three sides.

"It would be dark," one board member argued.

"And the acoustics would be bad," added another.

Frank tried to convince the board that with light from above and amber-glass ceiling lights there would be plenty of illumination, rain or shine. But the board wanted so many changes that he was almost ready to scuttle the whole project. Only after he made explanations with the help of a drawn-to-scale model did he win permission to go ahead.

The next problem was finding a contractor who would have imagination and initiative to carry out the plans. Finally Paul Mueller agreed to build the Temple.

For the walls concrete was cast in wooden forms. After the forms had been removed, exterior surfaces were washed to expose small gravel aggregates. In texture and effect the blocks resembled marble. The entrance to the auditorium was at the rear of the building via depressed passageways on either side.

The first time services were held in Unity Temple, Frank stayed away, worried that the skeptics might, after all, be displeased. He was entertaining his young daughter Frances when the telephone rang and congratulations began pouring in. Even the most stubborn opponent on the church board admitted that he could see and hear fine.

Between church and house building Frank found time to design a bank and take a trip to Japan. "Just like the prints," he reported when he returned.

In 1908 Mr. and Mrs. Avery Coonley came to confer about building a house at Riverside, Illinois. Wright was delighted when they told him that they had inspected a number of his houses and had seen in them the "countenance of principle."

The upper walls of the Coonley house were patterned with glazed ceramic tile laid in incised stucco. Although there were series of windows and French doors on three sides of the house, it still gave a sense of security. On a spread-out plan, the main functions of the house were in separate units but had connecting links. The living room, on the second floor to give a view of the Des Plaines River, had a soaring, spacious quality and an air of palatial luxury. A fern motif on the skylight was echoed by a mural on the wall. Windows were really metal grilles. Of the opinion that buildings should harmonize throughout like a musical composition, Wright planned not only furnishings, but the table service and even dresses for Mrs. Coonley.

Wright believed that a house with character would become more valuable as it grew older and said so in a long statement of his philosophy appearing in the *Architectural Record* of April, 1908. In the same article he wrote, "Principles are not evolved or invented by one man—they are perceived."

Although he was in love with his work, Wright took time out for relaxation, enjoying good food, good music and good company. He and Catherine went to dances, concerts and the theater. Because of his unrestrained character and aesthetic tastes, he had little in common with his Oak Park neighbors, but celebrities like Elbert Hubbard came to dinners or tea parties in the studio for long discussions of arts, crafts and philosophy.

Occasionally the family had a trip to the Valley, where they hiked, swam, and rode horseback. For riding in Chicago Wright had bought horses for John, Lloyd, and Frances, and a black, five-gaited saddlehorse, Kano, for himself. He also owned one of the first automobiles in Oak Park, a Stoddard Dayton sport roadster dubbed the Yellow Devil, which police threatened to confiscate because it could go sixty miles an hour.

Evenings were often given over to music. Cellist Lloyd alternately played and conducted the family orchestra composed of John, who played violin; Frances, piano; and David, flute. Catherine the second sang, and Llewellyn, as soon as he was old enough, plucked a guitar.

On most holidays Wright was as gay as the children, but the

Fourth of July was a solemn occasion. After explaining to the children that the flag stood for courage, truth and purity, he would hoist it dramatically. However, increasing responsibilities meant fewer and fewer hours with the family.

One of Wright's most important houses in 1909 was one for Frederick C. Robie, in Chicago. Built of tawny brick and stone with red tile roof and eaves of copper, it was a good example of prairie architecture. It had long, decklike balconies and superb masonry.

Wright's reputation was growing among architects abroad, but at home colleagues belittled his innovations, brushed aside his designs as impractical and ignored the solidity of his accomplishments. It was encouraging when German Kuno Francke, who was at Harvard as Roosevelt Exchange Professor in aesthetics, came to Oak Park to see Wright's work. Francke was impressed by Unity Temple, the Coonley and Robie houses, and other dwellings, and he urged Frank to come to Germany where he would be appreciated. "Fifty years will pass before your people are ready for you," he said.

In a way the idea of going to Germany was a tempting one. Wright had always loved the music of Bach and Beethoven and the writings of Goethe and Schiller. But he didn't speak German and the work he was doing seemed challenging, and so he declined. But before Kuno left there were long, stimulating conversations. They laughed together when Wright told the story of a Chicagoan who had said Chicago wasn't much on culture now but when the city did get after it they'd make culture hum.

Shortly after Francke's return to Germany Wright had a letter from Ernst Wasmuth, a Berlin publisher of art works, offering to publish an illustrated record of his building achievements. Would Wright come to supervise the publication? Busy with plans for City National Bank and Hotel at Mason City, Iowa, he declined again.

About this time everything went wrong for him. As he became increasingly absorbed in his work, Catherine became increasingly absorbed in motherhood. Once gay, she became irritable and impatient and seemed not to understand his dedication to his work. No harsh words were exchanged, but within himself Frank had the

Coonley House, Riverside, Illinois

growing conviction that a marriage in which aims were not mutual
was no good.

Lloyd often opposed his father, and even the younger children
defied Frank when he tried to discipline them for listening in on
the extension phone or disturbing him while he was interviewing
clients. One or another of the children was always becoming involved in a squabble, falling out of a tree, or cutting a finger.
Frances brought home stray animals that got underfoot. When the
children needed him, Frank offered his devotion unstintedly, but
he felt confused and tied down.

Crises multiplied. Despite handsome commissions, debts
hounded him. His intensity of effort to make income match outlay
resulted in a feeling of having lost his grip on his work. He loved
his children and he loved his home, but everything was impossibly
snarled. What could he do to work out the best possible life for
all concerned?

After Catherine had first agreed, then at the end of a year refused, to grant Wright a divorce, he decided the alternative was
voluntary exile. Perhaps away from the family for a time he could
re-establish values.

On the spur of the moment he decided he'd go to Germany and
supervise the portfolio Wasmuth wanted to publish. To raise
money for the trip and provide for his family in his absence he
sold some prized Japanese prints and made a frenzied round of his
clients. Current projects he turned over to a young Chicago
architect Von Holst, who also fell heir to his draftsmen.

Lloyd was in college, Catherine and Frances in private schools
and John at Hillside Home School, where his aunts would see that
he received the best of training.

Three weeks after Wright had made his decision to leave he was
sitting in a cafe in Paris too homesick to care what he ate, if anything. It was late at night, and the day had been rainy and endless.
He was getting some slight consolation from the orchestral music
until the cellist began to play Simonetti's "Madrigale." At home
Lloyd had often played this while Wright accompanied. With a
lump in his throat Wright got up and strode out of the cafe. His
future seemed no less black than the night around him.

9 *ALONE AT TALIESIN*

FROM PARIS WRIGHT WENT ON TO GERMANY, WHERE HE WAS SUR-
prised to find architects extolling his achievements. The Wasmuth
Publishing House wanted him to provide explanatory material to
accompany illustrations of his buildings being included in their
projected portfolio. While preparing the manuscript Wright settled
down in Italy at a little cream-colored villa in Fiesole near the city
of Florence.

He also studied the sculpture, paintings, and architecture of the
country. For recreation he took long walks, reveling in the high
color of poppies, the deep silence of the woods.

On a side trip to Greece Wright visited the crumbling ruins of
buildings on the Acropolis in Athens. Standing amid the desolate
grandeur he tried to picture what it had been like in the days of
Pericles, with sculptors working on the Parthenon while the rap-
ping of hammers of stonecutters came down from the heights above.

He admired the mellowed marble glowing almost golden in the
sun, the masterful use of harmony and proportion, the unity between the Parthenon and its site.

But the Greeks had divorced form from function. Their buildings had been fashioned from outside inward. The way surfaces
had been overlaid with paint seemed to show a lack of appreciation of the natural materials and made the buildings seem false.
Much of the embellishment, Wright knew, had been added by the
Turks; but even so, the Greeks were capable of finer, truer architecture than these buildings.

Some time after his return to Fiesole, Frank had word that the Wasmuth publication would soon be released. A Berlin exhibition of his work had also been planned. The portfolio and exhibit had a great influence on young European architects ready to pledge themselves to new ideas.

His residence abroad made Wright an even more fervent nationalist and Midwesterner. However, after almost two years in Europe he returned to the United States only to be met by a barrage of unfavorable publicity criticizing his architectural philosophy and more particularly his lengthy desertion of his family.

Wright felt he could not return to Oak Park. Something he'd read of Ruskin's kept going through his mind: "An architect should live as little in cities as a painter—let him study what nature understands."

When Frank's mother offered him a rock-ledged, oak-studded piece of land in the Valley, land that had once been his grandfather's, he accepted it gratefully. Only a few miles from Spring Green, Wisconsin, it would be an ideal place to build a combination house and workshop.

As he stood looking out over lush green hills speculating on where to build, Frank recalled scenes from his childhood— Grandfather with Bible in one hand and shepherd's crook over his left forearm, riding on his horse Timothy; Lloyd-Jones expeditions to pick apples, plums, or currants like clusters of rubies. To the southeast in plain view was the Romeo and Juliet windmill. Below lay the Wisconsin River.

He'd call his place Taliesin, Wright decided, after a Welsh druid-bard who was a member of King Arthur's Round Table and sang the glories of Fine Art. Literally the Welsh word meant "shining brow."

Wright had come back from Europe more than ever convinced that buildings should harmonize with their surroundings. He'd use matching limestone with faint reds and yellows, wood that matched the trunks of the oaks on the hilltop. The house itself must show the application of the principle of organic architecture.

The term organic did not originate with Wright, but he had

evolved a new philosophy about it. "Organic" really meant a natural pattern with all parts related to the whole, the purpose of the building giving it its character.

For the construction of Taliesin neighboring farmers, using horsepower, hauled in stones from a local quarry. Country masons laid the stone while William Weston, a Spring Green carpenter intelligent and swift of hand, directed the work with wood. Instead of having the dwelling on the hilltop Frank wanted it to flow with the wooded landscape and take its lines from the crest. If a lovely tree stood in the way, the builders detoured around it. The house with its gently sloping roof and long bands of windows faced southwest over the Valley so that the sun would come into every room at some time during the day. Flanking it Wright planned stone courts with walks, steps and pools. For water supply he depended on a swift stream nearby from which water was pumped uphill by an hydraulic ram.

When winter struck, the snow made Taliesin look like a frosted palace. Wright's roof encouraged icicles which hung down like iridescent pendants six feet in length. Plastering had been finished, but there was other inside work to be done. As they laid cypress board floors workmen threw cord wood into the fireplaces to warm themselves. Since most of the laborers lived in neighboring towns they stayed overnight, going home only on the weekends. As soon as possible Wright set up shop in his Taliesin studio, really a series of four rooms—one large, three small. A bank of tall windows let in light from the north.

Although he was gaining a reputation as a gifted architect, clients were not streaming to Taliesin and it seemed advisable to open a Chicago office in the Orchestra Hall Building. Sometimes when he was in the city Wright would go after dark to his old home in Oak Park and walk up and down outside straining his ears for the voices of the children. Hearing laughter he would be reassured that they were all right.

Occasionally Frank would have one of the boys spend the night with him at the Congress Hotel, or he would take his daughters Catherine and Frances out to dinner at the Tip Top Inn.

When spring came, with lilacs and wild plum perfuming the

breeze and robins, scarlet tanagers, and warblers singing from sunrise to sunset, Frank went to Chicago as infrequently as possible. To landscape Taliesin he used plants and flowers native to the region—ferns, crocuses, harebells, wild geraniums and phlox.

Most of the furniture at Taliesin was hand made. Rugs were tan-colored flax, curtains a brown checkered fabric. Wright liked to have people around and invited his mother and married sisters Maginel and Jane for long visits. Several apprentices made the place their home, and occasionally architects came visiting from abroad.

One of these visitors in 1912 was Hendrik P. Berlage, from Holland. Designer of the Bourse in Amsterdam, he had insisted that twentieth-century architecture must be based on twentieth-century construction. Admiring Wright and his philosophy, he returned home to lecture on the merits of Wright's work.

That year a number of buildings were planned in the Orchestra Hall office—among them the neighborhood playhouse for Mrs. Coonley.

In the fall of 1913 Edward C. Waller, Jr., son of a former client of Wright's, came to him with an idea for a resort garden that would be attractive and in good taste. This would be a place to dance, but also a place to hear fine music. The idea appealed to Frank, particularly if he could use characteristically American architecture.

As yet Waller had no land and no money, but he was confident about getting both. Frank agreed to draw a plan and did so in a remarkably short time. Meanwhile Waller procured a three-acre tract of ground, previously Sans Souci Park, just below Chicago University, and engaged the services of Paul Mueller as contractor for building Midway Gardens.

Wright's plan, in which he attempted to correlate architecture, sculpture, and painting, called for a system of low terraces enclosed by promenades, loggias, and galleries and a Winter Garden to include a dance floor and dining area. Walls were to be of reinforced concrete and tan-colored brick with flat towers at the corners topped by trellises which in summer would support flowers and vines. At night they would be ablaze with lights.

Shouting through a megaphone Mueller energetically directed the mad activity of excavators, steam shovel operators, masons, brick layers, hod carriers and carpenters.

To assist him at Midway Gardens Wright sought the help of his son John, who was planning for a career in architecture. During Wright's jaunts to Taliesin John kept an eye on construction and took charge of the office in Orchestra Hall. Wright was enormously pleased by John's persistence and interest. A hard worker, the boy also exhibited high purpose and sensitivity to beauty.

As the Midway Gardens progressed, builders and sponsors were beset by problems. Waller, who had undertaken the project knowing funds were insufficient, had hoped to raise money through popular subscription, but results were not as anticipated. Labor squabbles erupted. A half dozen times the union held up work on one pretext or another. And Charlie Matthews, who was an employee in Waller's office and also a musician, opposed Wright's plan for the orchestra shell, contending that the acoustics would be faulty. He insisted on interviewing musicians across the country about it. In the end, by making some slight concessions, Wright won Matthews over.

As the date for opening drew near work went on night and day. Wright and John sometimes slept in the Gardens on a bed of shavings. Because of lack of money and of time, many things remained undone, but sponsors decided to try to open on schedule. How would Chicago respond, Frank wondered. Buildings were not in the classical form to which the public had been accustomed. Sculpture and painting had been subordinated to the structure and much of the art was abstract.

One day when the Midway Gardens were nearly finished, Frank and John were having a late lunch on the grounds. To save time John snatched occasional bites from a sandwich while he drew a mural. A long-distance call came for Frank.

"Fire at Taliesin!" he reported, hurrying back to John.

Jumping down from the scaffolding John called a cab and with

his father boarded the slow local train to Spring Green. Frank dreaded what he might see. Would all of Taliesin be in ashes?

On the train Wright was told by reporters that a Barbados servant he had employed had gone mad and tossed kerosene-soaked lighted torches into the dining room at Taliesin. As the alarmed occupants fled, the maniac had killed with an ax three house guests, a talented apprentice, the gardener, a workman, and the son of carpenter William Weston. Numb with horror, Wright felt as if he were trapped in a nightmare, except that from this there would be no relief of awakening.

The trip to Spring Grove seemed without end. At the station Frank's cousin Richard Lloyd-Jones met them. As they neared Taliesin a pall of smoke hovered over the countryside. Men ran about with lanterns and flashlights.

Where the living quarters had been yawned a chasm. Only the chimneys stood. But that loss was nothing compared to the loss of friends and companions. Next day drifts of smoke still rose from the ruins. The murderer, barely alive, was found hiding in the fire pot of the steam boiler.

The scar on the hillside was not as severe as the scar on Wright's life. Taliesin had seemed a bulwark, a refuge where he could find peace. Now it lay devastated, his companions dead. Relatives and friends urged Frank to go home with them, but wanting to see no one he decided to stay on in the studio which Will Weston, although injured while grappling with the madman, had managed to save by seizing the hose and playing water on the structure.

The silence, the lack of activity weighed on Frank as days passed. Unable to sleep restfully at night he would get up and go outside searching for comfort and understanding, for some answer to the question of why the tragedy had come to him. But all he found were fear, blackness, aloneness. No stars shone.

Fresh losses were constantly occurring to him. The German monographs had been such a success in Europe that publisher Wasmuth had sent five hundred copies for sale in America. All but thirty had been destroyed in the fire.

Despair kept Frank's imagination too dull for creative work. He lost his appetite and subsequently weight. Boils bedeviled him. His

Midway Gardens, Chicago, Illinois

only solace was in music. On the day of the fire some of the crowd attracted by the flames had thrown his grand piano out a window. For its broken legs Wright substituted blocks and had it set up in his studio.

Meanwhile Midway Gardens had opened. Thousands had poured in to marvel and acclaim, enjoying its gaiety and charm. Orchestra shell acoustics were perfect. Despite favorable reports Frank was troubled because lack of funds had prevented his carrying out the crowning artistic touches.

Eventually, oppressed by the charred ruins at Taliesin and by his memories, Wright returned to Chicago to live in a little place at 25 East Cedar Street. His mother offered to keep house for him, but he wanted an impersonal housekeeper. For months it seemed that he would never build again. But gradually his conviction grew that the lovely hillside in the Valley should not be left to desolation. Stone by stone a Taliesin II would rise out of the ashes of the first.

Although there were some changes in design, the plan was much the same. All over again workmen hauled wood and stones and began to build. By late 1915 Taliesin II stood finer than the first. This time a guest unit had been added for Frank's mother and his aged aunts. Aunts Nell and Jane had closed the Hillside School, but age had not deprived them of their warmth and wisdom. Wright's mother, her eyes flashing with vitality, was as alert as ever and deeply interested in his plans for building.

His work had come alive again, but much of the time he had a sense of impending disaster. Unexpectedly a Japanese commission, including architect Yoshitaki and the manager of the Imperial Hotel, Aisaku Hayashi, arrived at Taliesin. They had, they told Wright, been on a world-wide quest for an architect to build a new Imperial Hotel and they were impressed by what they had seen of his work.

Would he be interested, they asked, in building a hotel that would serve as a clearing house for guests of the Emperor and distinguished foreign visitors—a place where Japanese gentlemen, who did not receive strangers at home, could entertain. The hotel, in addition to the usual facilities, should include a banquet hall, a theater, a swimming pool, and private supper rooms.

Wright assured them that the project challenged him. Since the Columbian Exposition he had been interested in Japanese prints. Japanese art was among the purest and noblest in the world, he said, and in Japan he could learn more about their techniques. Besides, a change might give him a lift. During the week that the commission remained at Taliesin, Wright made a preliminary plan which Hayashi took back to Japan.

Months passed. Finally an official invitation came for Wright to build the Imperial Hotel. It would be an enormous task to plan a structure that would please both Japanese and foreigners. And there would be the problem of erecting a building that could withstand earthquakes. Wright had never tackled a project as formidable as this, but hard work might rescue him from the loneliness that had haunted him ever since the fire.

10 *THE MORNING LAND*

FULL OF ANTICIPATION FOR THE TRIP TO JAPAN, WRIGHT AND HIS son John embarked on the *Empress of Russia*, where they had a luxurious suite of rooms. When the ship dropped anchor in Yokohama, white birds and sampans with white sails manned by bronzed fishermen dotted the water.

On hand to meet Wright was Baron Okura, representing the Imperial Household. Although over eighty, he was hardy and lively and his hair was still jet black. There was nothing in the miles of peaceful countryside between the port city and Tokyo to indicate that Japan was at war with Germany. Thus far participation in World War I had been confined to a few forays against German-held islands in the Pacific.

Arriving in Tokyo Wright saw Japanese in western dress mingling with women in bright-colored kimonos who wore clogs over soft, fitted white cotton sock shoes. As soon as he set foot on the site for the Imperial Hotel he realized that the plans worked out at Taliesin wouldn't do. The building should harmonize with the Imperial Palace across the park from it, guarded by an ancient moat. Japanese traditions were worthy of respect, thought Wright; the structure should be suitable to the culture and environment. That would mean using native materials and hand methods as much as possible. This hotel must belong to the Japanese, yet be modern enough to provide maximum convenience for foreign visitors.

Another problem Wright had to take into consideration was

that in Japan steel rusts with fearful rapidity, because of humidity. The greatest problem, however, was the threat of earthquakes. Japan has more of them than any other country in the world.

Studying the behavior of earthquakes, Wright learned that the enormous weight of the Pacific Ocean straining against the earth crust of the islands of Japan opens fissures, permitting water to rush down to subterranean fires. The gas and steam created expand or explode internally. As underground rocks split, vibrations or convulsive waves go shuddering through the land in all directions from the center of the disturbance.

As a result of seismic shocks in the past, he knew, foundations had trembled and semi-rigid frameworks had weakened, cracked or even broken. Concrete shells had been wrenched off, exposing steel to the flames that always accompany quakes. Under intense heat steel will bend at riveted knees and collapse and in this way steel buildings had often become death traps. No Japanese architect had as yet evolved an earthquake-proof structure.

From his research Wright concluded that protection against earthquakes lay in resiliency, lightness, and flexibility of foundations and superstructure. Studying the five-hundred-by-three-hundred-foot site for the Imperial Hotel, he discovered that beneath eight feet of cheeselike soil lay soft mud. The surface soil had no carrying power, and what could any architect do with a sea of mud?

An idea struck Wright that it might be possible by use of concrete piers to float the hotel on mud in the way a battleship floats on the ocean. Instead of fighting the quake, the building would rock with it; but a requisite would be a flexible foundation. Wright ordered holes dug into the ground and then had concrete poured in. Later he tried the technique of driving tapered piles down, and then, as soon as the pile was withdrawn, having the workmen dump in the concrete.

Soon pile drivers dotted the area, each operated by a band of singing women who pulled on ropes to lift and drop the driving head. Over the heads of the concrete piers only two feet apart Wright had platforms built. On each of these, sand bags were piled and wire was strung about six inches above the tops of the piers.

Using this device he could estimate how much weight each pier could support and how much each settled, and then compute the diameter and length of piers needed.

— The experimentation with shock absorbers had taken a year, but Frank had come up with a strikingly original solution of a tough architectural problem. His plan now was to divide the building into sections sixty feet long, which would be a safe limit for temperature cracks in reinforced concrete. Sections would be joined together. To insure stability the floor would be cantilevered on the platforms topping the piers.

Wright had previously used cantilevers, projecting beams or girders fixed at one end to a rigid support, but never so extensively as this. Through these the floor could be stabilized in the manner of a waiter carrying a tray on his outstretched hand. This would permit the balancing of load against load and give the structure flexibility.

The Western Society of Engineers warned that such a scheme for a foundation was unsafe. Convinced that they were wrong, Wright went ahead with other details. Because Tokyo buildings were top-heavy with weighty roof tiles that were a menace in an earthquake, Wright decided to use sheet copper. For the walls he wanted something light. Oya, a greenish-colored, leopard-spotted lava stone resembling travertine, seemed to be the answer. Its abundance would make it inexpensive, and combined with handmade brick it would be very effective.

The building committee, which included bankers and industrialists as well as representatives of the royal family, objected to the use of oya as being too cheap and common.

"It would not be enduring," authorities contended.

Wright insisted and in the end won out. During the planning it was not essential that he remain in Japan, where he found the climate taxing. Because of the humidity the heat was oppressive, the cold, accompanied by winds or stifling mists, penetrating. Besides, the endless tests and the strains of interpreting his goals where a language barrier existed had worn him down. Leaving John in charge, he sailed for the United States, taking with him several Japanese students of architecture to help with plans.

However, Wright later fired John via a cablegram because he deducted twelve hundred dollars from a fee earmarked for his father before turning it over to him. The sum was due John in salary and he was tired of lavish meals, treats, or occasional bills his father tucked in his pockets as substitutes for regular payments for services. John returned to Chicago to open his own office.

When Wright went back to Japan with his completed plans no one wanted to tackle the unusual job. Once more Wright appealed to Paul Mueller. At Oya near Nikko Wright bought a lava quarry where workmen loaded slabs of oya on rafts and floated them by sea to Tokyo and then by canal to the site of the hotel.

As construction proceeded, the Japanese were wary. Foreigners disapproved of the concessions to Oriental taste. Because Wright taught the natives to do their own work, American construction companies were hostile. The seismograph, never still, was a constant reminder of the menace against which he worked. Sometimes he would awaken at night with the strange sensation of being at sea.

Wright spent long hours at his drafting board and on the job overseeing workmen, but there was also time for relaxation in the apartment he had been permitted to build in the annex that housed guests while the hotel was under construction. On the main floor of the apartment he had a living room with fireplace and balcony of dwarf trees and flowers, a bedroom, and a small dining room where meals were brought from the hotel kitchen by the Japanese boy who served him. A narrow stairway led to a roomy upstairs bedroom-studio.

Wright amused himself reading or playing the piano and rambling around Tokyo, and enjoyed entertaining or being entertained by Tokyo friends. When visiting in Japanese houses he usually wore the native costume. He at first admired the elaborate ritual of the high tea ceremony, and sensed a hidden spiritual meaning that he wanted to understand; but after observing it several times he found the repetition tiresome. Boredom and soreness of his knees induced him to avoid the ordeal whenever possible.

One evening Wright was entertained at Baron Okura's. The

universal heater, the *hibachi*, a round vessel filled with white ashes into which several sticks of lighted charcoal had been thrust, was inadequate. Wright, who had not adopted the Japanese custom of wearing long underwear, was so cold that he couldn't enjoy the fascinating nineteen-course dinner, which included fish soup, bowls of rice, and curiously designed sweets.

After dinner the baron invited his guests to have Turkish coffee in the Korean room, where a red felt drugget covered the floor mats. No heating was visible, but Frank could feel a cozy warmth. When he commented on this fact to the Harvard graduate who interpreted for the baron, he explained that Korean room meant one warmed by means of heated air forced through tile ducts under the floor. The fire was actually outside the house. This would be an idea to take back to the States, thought Wright. He had always detested ugly heating fixtures. And he resolved that heating elements should be installed beneath the floors of the bathrooms at the Imperial.

Frank had expected to do a lot of sightseeing, but streets in Tokyo were narrow, drivers reckless, and traffic rules ineffective. Because rural roads were potholed, muddy and poorly maintained, he drove the Overland less and less, but when he did get out into the countryside he enjoyed the terraced fields and profuse, brilliant flowers with snowy Fujiyama as a backdrop. Everyone seemed friendly, from children with babies on their backs to indigo-clad toilers in the rice paddies.

Wright deplored imitations of western architecture but was fascinated by the many shrines with elaborate tile roofs and houses built with all the naturalness of a turtle's shell. In Japanese houses, where shape was determined by the size of the floor mats, he could see the influence of Lao Tze, who before the time of Jesus had declared that the nobility of a building did not consist in four walls and a roof, but was determined by the space within. Wright had once imagined himself to be the creator of the idea of building from inside outward, but now he saw that neither he nor Lao Tze had created a principle, but merely perceived one that was eternal and therefore universal.

The interiors of Japanese houses had easily removable sliding panels, and all furnishings not in actual use were stored in the "go-down." Even the humblest house had a *tokonoma*, a recess devoted to fine art. One day it might contain a single painting, another the saying of a poet or a floral arrangement related to the day, season, or occasion. The spotlessly clean kitchens were like well-ventilated studios.

Wright knew it would be out of the question for Americans to live in the cold, papery Japanese houses, but they could borrow Japanese integrity and live in houses disciplined by high ideals. Another thing he liked about their architecture was the treatment of wood. Instead of overlaying with paint the natural beauty and wavelike contours of good grained wood, native builders revealed or heightened them.

Because Wright was departing from ordinary construction routines, he had to conduct endless tests at the site for the Imperial Hotel. For the plumbing he decided to use pipes of lead with easy bends set in trenches. His hope was that a quake would flex but not break them. Climate was a drawback in the building progress. During the rainy season it seemed that the rain came from the ground up.

There were also difficulties with workmen. Presumably Hayashi San was in direct charge of the six hundred artisans, but he lacked knowledge of western techniques. Although Wright had modified many of his original intentions in order to accommodate native methods, some use of mechanical devices seemed expedient, but laborers resisted them. Instead of using hoists they would carry heavy loads on their backs. Abandoned planes lay buried under chips. Wright, who was direct and outspoken, was often frustrated by Oriental obliqueness and guile.

Holidays kept interrupting construction. The workmen did not take Sunday off, but every fortnight there was a double holiday, the celebration of which was so strenuous that they often required an additional day for recovery. Complications also arose with families living at the site.

But on the job the Japanese were tireless, deft, patient, and resourceful. As construction on the Imperial progressed, the workmen became absorbed in the project and were loyal to Wright.

Walls of the hotel were double. The outer one of handmade brick and oya was wide and thick at the base, tapering at the top. For the inside wall Wright used fluted, hollow brick. Concrete reinforced by steel rods filled and bound them together.

Because of all the unknowns involved, Wright had been unable to make a specific estimate of cost at the beginning of the project, but now it was evident that he'd need an additional three and a half million yen. From the first, Baron Okura had been untiring in his patience and understanding, but dissatisfaction and disagreement had developed among the board of directors.

The day Wright was to go before the board to ask for more money he was not feeling well and as a consequence was depressed over the possible outcome. Usually the meetings had been pleasant, but today Asano-san, who represented the shipping interests, looked perturbed. In the piercing eyes under shaggy brows hostility lurked as Baron Okura explained the reason for the shortage of funds. The board's reluctance to grant the additional yen was not helped by the pessimism of long-bearded Wakai.

Feeling worse by the moment as the hectic discussion went on, Wright was almost ready to scuttle the project when Baron Okura, ordinarily gentle and affable, suddenly rose to his feet and pounded on the table. If the directors wouldn't back Wright, he declared, he would do so with his own personal fortune.

As the directors filed out without a word, Frank gratefully extended his hand to Baron Okura, but he wished he'd won the loyalty of the others.

11 SONG TO HEAVEN

DISGRUNTLED MEMBERS OF THE BOARD CONTINUED TO GIVE FRANK trouble. At intervals, depressed by their spying and by homesickness, he would book passage for the United States, taking with him to Taliesin art treasures, mostly prints, which he'd been collecting avidly. The imitative ones being turned out by contemporary artists didn't interest him, but he admired the sweeping lines against the mellow texture of rice paper in the originals of Hiroshige, Kiyonaga and Utamaro. These ranged from soft colors to bright ones or primitive blacks.

Even America's involvement in World War I did not keep Wright from crossing the Pacific, since operations had been largely confined to battles in Europe and submarine activity in the Atlantic. While Wright was on one of his visits home William Spaulding came to his office in Chicago to examine some of the prints and paid ten thousand dollars for a portfolio of them. A few days later he invited Wright to his own home in Boston and there offered to put to Wright's credit in a Tokyo bank twenty thousand dollars to buy additional ones.

Upon his return to Japan, Wright consulted an art connoisseur and let it be known that he wanted originals. Hitherto the prints had not been appreciated in the United States or Japan and could be bought cheaply. Now prices soared.

Meanwhile Wright had taken on a building project in addition to the Imperial—a house for Aline Barnsdall in Los Angeles. On a trip home in 1917 he had seen the Olive Hill site and conferred with his client on a plan for a dwelling pre-named Hollyhock House, because she had selected that flower as a motif in the ornament. Wright wanted to design a place that would have no resemblance to the "sentimental bosh" current in California architecture. It should embody characteristics of the region, yet fit the personality of its owner, who was interested in dramatics.

Wright found it hard to get his ideas carried out with an ocean between him and building operations. The contractor's inability to interpret the design necessitated an exchange of telegrams. Several problems arose about which Frank wanted to consult with Miss Barnsdall, but she, infected by wanderlust, was usually unavailable at the critical moment. While he was supervising placement of oya at the Imperial, she might be in Hollywood, but when Wright was in Hollywood to check progress she might be in Bombay or Barcelona. Misunderstandings developed among architect, owner, and contractor, resulting in angry exchanges and makeshift substitutions. Finally Wright's son Lloyd, a promising young architect, came to his rescue and kept an eye on the construction.

As the lower stories of the Imperial were completed, workmen began immediately to do woodwork, install copper fixtures and make furniture on the site. For generations the Japanese had been sitting and eating on the floor; now Wright patterned furniture according to western usages, but made the tables lower and followed the Japanese custom of keeping everything not needed at the moment out of sight.

Wright went to Peking, China, to let contracts for hand-woven rugs. In the company of Dr. Ku Hung Ming who, although an Oxford graduate, wore a cue curled up under his red mandarin cap, he visited palaces and temples, including the blue-tiled Temple of Heaven, while writer and sage Dr. Ku expounded upon the culture of Japan and China.

On the job again, Wright was making considerable progress in winning the confidence of the Japanese when news came that Californians, alarmed by the influx of Japanese labor, were demanding restrictions on immigration. Radicals were referring to the Japanese as an inferior race. There were indignation meetings in Tokyo, and Wright was not allowed abroad without protection.

Then friction developed over a pool he had designed as a feature of the entrance court at the Imperial. Wright's idea had been that it would be a safety measure as well as a feature to add charm. Fires following an earthquake were often more damaging than the vibrations themselves. Even with the city water supply disrupted, the hotel pool would be a defense against conflagration. But the cost, forty thousand yen, disturbed the directors.

"Why not eliminate the pool?" one of them suggested.

Wright told Okura privately that unless the pool stayed he wished to be released from the agreement for the completion of the hotel. After he'd returned to his apartment and no word came, Wright was afraid that he'd lost not only the argument but a friendship as well.

Eventually he got the pool and the Imperial Household demonstrated their respect for him by conferring upon him the title of Kenchiko Ho, High Builder.

When Frank became ill from the combined effects of climate, overwork and strain, his mother, now eighty, but possessed of a pioneering spirit, crossed the Pacific to be near him. Her presence was steadying. All of Frank's friends took her sightseeing and the Japanese made much of her. For the Emperor's garden party he designed clothes for her that would suit the occasion—a silver and gray dress, a long purple cloak, and a small violet bonnet like a close crown over her white hair. Although involved in an auto accident later, she was able to return home when the time came that she had set for herself.

For diversion and also for profit, Wright resumed his search for prints. In addition to ferreting out items for private collectors, he had a commission from the Chicago Art Institute and a contract with fastidious art collector Howard Mansfield, treasurer of the Metropolitan Museum in New York.

Some natives disliked selling prints to a foreigner, but money was scarce and Wright was persuasive. One day a dealer gave him a tip on some prints he said might be available in a home near Nikko. Wright journeyed to that city and rode in a ricksha to the

house hidden in the woods. There he found a superb collection, including a large-size Harunobu printed in gold leaf on heavy crimped paper, and he bought the collection for fifty thousand dollars.

On his next voyage home he took the masterpieces with him. After having them mounted and classified, he delivered them to Mansfield, but several months after he was back in Tokyo, Frank had a cablegram saying that a number of the prints showed pinpricks.

Wright was aghast, but felt that in a way it served him right, for he'd really had a share in the West's looting of the Orient. Investigation proved that some unscrupulous Japanese had worked out an ingenious system whereby through soaking old prints and then using pinpricks and wood blocks, they could effect accurate reproductions. But museums wanted only originals.

Good prints were now becoming scarce, and to replace the Mansfield collection seemed out of the question, so Wright proposed that when he returned to America, Mansfield should come to Taliesin and take his choice of his own collection.

Determined to put an end to the production of hoaxes, Wright appealed to the authorities, who jailed the ringleader of the operators and would have meted out a death penalty had not Wright intervened with the suggestion that the dealer be released but forbidden to deal in prints.

As work on the hotel continued, Wright encountered opposition from an unexpected quarter. An article sponsored by the American Institute of Architecture and published in a Tokyo paper declared that the Imperial Hotel was an insult to American architecture and that the building would tumble in the first major quake. But Wright's friends, the Hanis, gave him a vote of confidence by asking him to design the Tokyo School for Girls.

Around noon one day in April 1922, Wright was in his workroom above the promenade entrance of the hotel when a jolt of bomblike intensity, accompanied by an unearthly rumble, sent the young men of his staff sprawling. While they were scrambling to their feet Wright had the sensation of the bottom dropping from beneath the building. Before he could think what to do he

Imperial Hotel, Tokyo, Japan

was knocked down by workmen rushing from the room intent on saving their lives. As he lay on the floor, dazed and perspiring, he could actually see the "ground swell" pass through the building. Grinding noises and thunderous crashes convinced him that at least part of the hotel had been twisted apart. There was the sound of falling brick, and then silence.

Shakily Wright got to his feet and stared speechlessly at the one assistant who had stayed beside him. Together they went outside. Across the street stood crowds of white-faced workmen, rigid and voiceless. Suddenly bells clanged and men sprang into action to fight fires that had broken out across the city. Women snatched crying children out of the streets.

Dreading what he might find, Wright made a frenzied inspection of the hotel. The sounds of crashing brick had been caused by the collapsing chimneys of the *old* Imperial. Transits put on the foundation showed no deviation, although this was the worst quake Tokyo had been subjected to for fifty-two years. Wright's work had been tested and found adequate.

As the time for leaving drew near, he experienced both satisfaction and displeasure. The Imperial Hotel certainly was in tune with the land and the people and he had built an earthquake-proof building that would stand as a monument for generations. But in a way he'd been deflected from his goal: the structure didn't look much like a product of the machine age. But the Imperial Household was delighted. Really an aggregate of buildings, the main part was a squatty structure three stories high, elaborated with parapets, and with special masses equivalent to an ordinary building of seven stories. The simplicity of detail and elegance of execution made the Imperial look like a spacious palace. Slim, fluted, almost gold-colored brick blended with turquoise copper and greenish-yellow oya in a distinctive and beautiful harmony.

Two five-hundred-foot-long wings contained guest rooms. A promenade sixteen feet above sidewalk level connected these with the dining room, the parlor and a theater that seated a thousand people. The hotel, with separate entrances for cars and rickshas, was flanked by a garden court, terraces, and bridges that seemed

Imperial Hotel, Tokyo, Japan

to float. "Characterized by *shibui*, the reward of earnest contemplation," said the Japanese.

Interior details were lavish. For the dining room Wright had even designed the china. In the ballroom great trusses were elaborately decorated with abstract designs in color. Carved panels represented conventionalized peacocks. "Wonderful rhythm and color," said some. Others thought the ornamentation overdone, with the repetition of peacocks not unlike too-insistent drum beats. The establishment also included a private dining room, a bazaar, and a swimming pool.

Although one wing was still incomplete, Wright decided that since the second would be a duplication of the first his services were no longer needed, and he prepared to return to the States. His fee was three hundred and eighty thousand dollars, a sum supplemented by Baron Okura and others as a sign of appreciation. Most of it Frank spent on Japanese or Chinese prints, fabrics, lacquerware, pottery, sculpture and screens of rare quality.

There was a series of farewell luncheons, teas and dinners. On the day that he was to sail he felt deflated when there seemed to be no one around to say good-by. But in the entrance court, crowds of workmen, from sweepers to foremen, crowded around laughing and shaking hands. A number of them followed his car to the station shouting, "*Banzai Wrieto-san, banzai.*"

Wright went by train to Yokohama to take his boat. At the dock sixty foremen had assembled to bid him farewell. Their shouts followed the ship as it sailed down the blue waters of the bay. Frank stood on deck until the foremen and calm, majestic Fujiyama were no longer visible.

Japan might be gone from sight but not from memory. The everyday singing of the human spirit he'd found among her people, their "song to heaven," would be with him always, as haunting as a plaintive tune played on the strings of a samisen.

12 *TESTED BY QUAKE, FLOOD AND FIRE*

WHILE IN JAPAN WRIGHT HAD BECOME INTERESTED IN THE SHINTO philosophy of clean hands, clean heart, clean purposes. These ideals, he thought on his voyage homeward, could be applied to architecture. The best buildings would be those coming out of clean use of machines and clean workmanship with a simplicity not just hand-felt but heart-felt.

Upon his arrival in the United States he was too exhausted to make a practical application of these principles. Knowing heavy demands would be made on him as soon as he returned to the Chicago office, he decided he would first spend some time in California, where, if he took on any projects, Lloyd would be at hand to help him. Temporarily he settled down in a studio on Olive Hill, Los Angeles.

One of his first activities was a check-up on Hollyhock House, which had finally been completed. Around it Aline Barnsdall had planted eucalyptus, pines, and exotic flowers. It was a proud house even if mistakes had been made in construction. The abstract hollyhocks were very effective as ornamentation capping the solid masses of concrete.

Reactions of the streams of visitors who came to see it were varied. Artists approved it; local architects ridiculed it. In the use made of mass some thought they saw the influence of old Mayan architecture.

Although Wright had returned to America a number of times during the years he'd been supervising the construction of the

Imperial Hotel, he had been out of touch with architectural advances. World War I had brought developments in industry, science, and new materials which were having a tremendous impact.

In Europe, where there had been enormous destruction of property, only a few architects chose to rebuild in the old classical styles. Many of the younger men had come under the influence of the brilliant Dr. Walter Gropius, who shortly after the end of World War I in 1919 had founded the Bauhaus, a school of design at Weimar, which was to become a laboratory for relating the ideas of artists, designers and architects to the needs of industry and building. The Bauhaus advocated pure geometrical composition and large plain surfaces. Already these concepts were beginning to take hold in America.

Almost no one agreed with Wright's ideas, although in *Architectural Record* for April 1924 his Imperial Hotel was cited as "the high water mark thus far attained by any modern architect." But in a book of architects compiled in 1922 by the Educational Committee of the American Institute of Architects, his name was not even mentioned.

Driving around Los Angeles in a custom-designed Cadillac which attracted bystanders whenever he parked, Wright didn't approve the trend to Spanish medievalism. What he characterized as fraudulent, cheap opulence depressed him. Nor did he endorse the city's bid for bigness. In a pamphlet he had printed and distributed mostly in California, he declared that cities were becoming more and more unfit as living places and that skyscrapers, dangerous to construct, operate, and maintain, were a menace to welfare. The pamphlet did nothing to increase his popularity.

While still at the Olive Hill studio, Wright spent much time and energy on designing a block-square building for the National Life Insurance Company and was all set to supervise actual construction when he received word that the company had failed.

Deep in research on new uses for old materials, he was only momentarily discouraged by the reverse. Opposed to the practice of many architects who imported foreign woods and marble, he sought techniques that would proclaim the beauty and dignity of

Barnsdall House, Los Angeles, California

local materials and at the same time be suitable to the terrain and climate.

Now he was challenged by the idea of letting steel enter inert masses of concrete to give it new usefulness. Concrete blocks with steel in their joints would be light, yet rugged and enduring. One big advantage was that they could be made right at the scene of the construction and shaped into any size desired. Since concrete had plasticity it could be given appropriate texture and artistic design that would keep it from ugliness.

When Mrs. George Millard, an artist with a manner as direct as her frank blue eyes, came to Wright about building a house in Pasadena, he asked her if she'd let him test out his ideas in using textured concrete blocks. She assented to a plan for a house with double concrete walls and a hollow space between. Living room and kitchen would be on the roof deck, the bedroom on garden level.

With a ravine for the site, Wright had a fine opportunity to stress kinship of structure and ground. Lloyd assisted on the house, which was to be called La Miniatura. But from the first the project seemed ill-fated. While Mrs. Millard was in Europe the contractor disappeared. The money allotted for the building was two-thirds spent, but the house was only half finished. Workmen kept coming in, staying a short time, then fading away.

Faced by debts, duns, liens and false charges, Wright borrowed six thousand dollars to finish the balconied dwelling which finally stood tall and lovely between two eucalyptus trees. The blocks textured in varying but harmonizing patterns were beautiful, and the ravine had become a terraced garden with a pool reflecting the trees.

After Mrs. Millard moved in, a torrential rain sent a flood roaring down the ravine and although the deluge failed to dislodge La Miniatura, it left solid mud on the lower floors. Later, because of shoddiness in construction, the roof leaked. In the end, however, all the problems were solved and La Miniatura justified Wright's belief that sticking to ideals will bring success although contractors pull out, workmen bungle, and bankers balk.

One night in September 1923 word came that an earthquake, the

Millard House, Pasadena, California

worst in intensity and duration in Japan's history, had virtually wiped out Tokyo and Yokohama. Remembering the first time of testing, Wright was sure that the Imperial Hotel had escaped— but what of Baron Okura and other friends? Unable to sleep, he paced around restlessly.

In succeeding days, efforts to establish communication with friends were futile. The third night after the disaster a reporter from the Los Angeles *Examiner* called to relay the news that the Imperial Hotel had been destroyed. There were so many buildings in Tokyo called Imperial that Frank was confident a mistake had been made. "If anything is above ground in the city, it is the hotel," he told the reporter. But as grisly details of a hundred and forty-two thousand casualties poured in, he wondered if anything had survived. In occasional moments of doubt he pictured his structure engulfed in a yawning chasm.

Ten days after the disaster a telegram came to the Olive Hill studio. FOLLOWING WIRELESS RECEIVED FROM TOKYO TODAY HOTEL STANDS UNDAMAGED AS MONUMENT OF YOUR GENIUS HUN-DREDS OF HOMELESS PROVIDED BY PERFECTLY MAINTAINED SERVICE CONGRATULATIONS.

OKURA.

Wright's strict adherence to sound principles of construction, planned resilience, low center of gravity, and conscientious work-manship had saved lives. That the Imperial had survived the upheaval brought great joy.

When letters came through, Wright was relieved to learn that none of his friends had been harmed, but both of Baron Okura's houses had been destroyed, as well as the museum he had given Tokyo. Julius Floto, structural engineer for the Imperial, wrote that the hotel had been shaken like a toy, but that there had been no dislocation. Several stone figures in the Imperial garden had literally sunk into the ground, but in the structure itself not one pane of glass had been broken. The plumbing and heating systems had remained intact.

After fire had broken out, the hotel remained an island of safety. Fleeing past hundreds of dead lying in the streets, Japanese mothers had come there with their children. City water mains had been disrupted, but hotel employees had formed bucket brigades and used water from the pools in the garden to wet down window sashes and frames so that they did not ignite when a conflagration swept toward the hotel.

In an article in the *Architectural Record* of February 1924, Wright's former employer, Louis Sullivan, wrote that the Imperial Hotel had survived only because it had been "thought-built."

During the California interlude Frank had married Miriam Noel, a Parisian born sculptress, having been granted a divorce from Catherine some time previously. The brilliant, sophisticated Miriam had many interests that matched Frank's, but was given to periods of serious emotional disturbances.

Wright, leaving the Los Angeles field to his son Lloyd, looked forward to a return to Taliesin with Miriam at his side. But once there she was not interested in the rural setting, hikes, horseback riding or swimming and soon left for Chicago.

Loneliness plagued Wright. His aunts Nell and Jane had died while he was in Japan. Now his mother was gone too. But young architects, attracted by what they'd heard about Wright and Taliesin, were coming at intervals and some stayed on as apprentices. Two of the most promising were Richard Neutra and Werner Moser. Werner was the son of Herr Professor Moser of Zurich, a leading European architect, and Richard Neutra was from Vienna. Coming to Taliesin at a time when Wright was gone, Neutra had camped down with the apprentices he found there. He and his wife Dione had a son, as did Werner and his wife Sylvia. Wright enjoyed the children and found them entertaining. Dione, Sylvia, and the other wives, dubbed the Merry Wives of Taliesin, helped out with Frank's domestic needs. Werner played the violin and Dione played cello and sang, so there were evenings of music.

Wright was also very fond of a Japanese apprentice, Kameki and his wife, Nobu. Once, taking the two of them, with Nobu looking like a petite doll in her Japanese dress, he went to call on Zona Gale, whose book *Lula Betts* had impressed him. He disliked her Colonial style house, but found her completely charming and subsequently met a number of celebrities at her home.

Off and on through the years Frank had corresponded with

Louis Sullivan, for whom things had gone badly. Riding on the crest of popularity at the time of the opening of the Chicago Auditorium, he had later been virtually thrust aside during the depression of the 1890's and the classical revival following the Columbian Exposition. His caustic speech had lost him would-be clients. Under the impact of drinking, his health had failed, his work faltered. Reduced almost to starvation, he had turned to writing, often vague and mystical in content.

Now whenever Wright was in Chicago he tried to visit Sullivan, providing him with necessities or little treats like the strong black coffee he craved. At times Sullivan's concern about a livelihood would overcome his high courage. But on other days his eyes burned as brightly as ever; the old gleam of humor would come and go, and although his hands trembled and breath control wavered, he would insist on reading excerpts from his *Autobiography of an Idea*, with a show of buoyancy and pride. He could still lash out against architects who yielded to the mercenary hurly-burly.

In the office Sullivan had called him Wright, but now it was always Frank. One day when Wright went he found Sullivan very ill. On his table was a bound copy of the *Autobiography* which he wanted to autograph, saying, "The first copy to you."

But he was too weak to write his signature. Before leaving him Wright did everything he could think of to insure Sullivan's comfort. He never saw him again, for Sullivan died April 14, 1924. Aside from the book he had no valuable personal possessions except a daguerrotype of his mother, which he had instructed his nurse to give to Frank.

There was little time to brood over the injustice of Sullivan's fate, for Wright was involved in projects and by visitors streaming to Taliesin and the Chicago office. One of these was the well-known German architect Eric Mendelsohn. Vital and imaginative, Mendelsohn had an exuberant optimism and enthusiasm for his work and he and Wright agreed on the necessity of a return to nature for architectural inspiration. Mendelsohn was obviously profoundly impressed by Wright's philosophy and by his buildings.

A summer visitor at Taliesin one day in 1925 was Alexander Woollcott. Shortly after the author had left, a thunderstorm came up. As he went to his supper Wright had noticed the intensity of the zigzag lightning and when he came down from the detached room where his meal had been served, he saw smoke pouring from his bedroom.

"Fire!" Wright yelled hoarsely. But at the moment no one was around except Frank's driver, Mel, and his apprentice, Kameki.

The flames whipped by a high wind threatened once more to destroy Taliesin.

13 BUILDINGS PLANNED BUT NEVER BUILT

FOR TWO HOURS WRIGHT AND HIS ASSISTANTS BATTLED THE FIRE. Just when they thought it had been extinguished there was a crackling in the dead space under the roof and flames leaped up anew. The blaze, accompanied by clouds of smoke and sparks, attracted neighbors. With singed hair and smoke-filled lungs Wright directed operations of some who volunteered to help.

After the living quarters of Taliesin had been destroyed, the weary firefighters, discouraged by the dwindling water supply, lay down to get their breath. "No use trying to save the work rooms," they panted. But Frank persisted.

Suddenly thunder pealed. Into the sheet of fire rain fell with a hissing noise. The workrooms were saved, but the rest of Taliesin had been so completely consumed that plate glass windows lay like pools in the ashes. Of Wright's personal effects only the soggy, smoke-saturated garments he had on remained. Most of the rare Japanese prints were gone. The desolation in Frank's heart was as immense as the destruction surrounding him. Everything seemed lost and there was no one to turn to for comfort. By now most of the Valley relatives had died or gone elsewhere. But through the years Frank's conviction had been growing that every problem carried its own solution—a solution reached only by sincere devotion to truth.

A few days after the disaster Wright began clearing away debris. The fire, he knew now, had been caused by a short circuit in a telephone. In the ashes he stumbled on fragments of basalt from a

Wei stone and Ming pottery turned to the color of bronze by the intensity of the blaze. These he put aside to incorporate in the masonry of Taliesin III, already taking shape in his mind.

Working in his studio, Wright made forty drawings before he finally got what he wanted. This time he would use more and better building materials, more and better workmen, more intelligent execution.

Through tenacious effort Taliesin III emerged early in 1925. In the living room Frank had achieved a dramatic effect with a low-ceilinged entry leading into a soaring, almost cathedral-like space with overhanging balconies and changes in ceiling line. After the restoration, apprentices came once more.

But the next few years brought distractions and confusion into Frank's personal affairs. Adverse publicity cut down on commissions. When the depression came, lovely houses and prophetic buildings never got beyond the drawing-board stage because the person or firm requesting the design lacked money to carry through.

Another factor in Frank's unemployment was that many Americans still venerating classical form found his styles incomprehensible. Abroad this was not the case. *Wendingen*, a Dutch-English-German fine art publication edited by Th. J. Widejveld, dedicated a volume to his works. The Flemish Académie Royale d' Anvers and the Académie Royale des Beaux Arts in Belgium bestowed honorary membership on him.

Financially Wright was in deep trouble. Replacement of the worthless, pinpricked Japanese prints had cost him thirty thousand dollars. The fire and a fantastic sum of money Miriam demanded in exchange for a divorce further drained his resources. Salaries had to be paid apprentices, and Taliesin III, already mortgaged, was expensive to maintain.

Wright sold some of the remaining Japanese prints, but that was only a temporary expedient. Turning to writing he did a series of articles for *Architectural Record* on the nature of materials, dealing in turn with concrete, wood, and sheet metal. For a time he stayed with his married sister Maginel in New York.

When, at Taliesin once more, Frank failed to meet payments

due, he received a legal notice that he was to leave the premises. He was now without a home and without a job. Auspiciously a telegram came from Albert McArthur, who had been an apprentice in the Oak Park studio, asking him if he could come out to Phoenix to help with the Arizona Biltmore Hotel, which he had been commissioned to build.

Wright accepted the offer. The work afforded a livelihood, but was not very interesting, because most of his suggestions, which were unusual, were disregarded. But he enjoyed the hospitality accorded him.

While helping with the Biltmore Frank met Dr. Alexander Chandler, who had built his own town of Chandler on a mesa about twenty-two miles from Phoenix. Wright admired Chandler's discriminating judgment and independence. To him Chandler confided his dream of building a winter resort for millionaires to be called San Marcos in the Desert.

After seeing the site, Frank was wildly enthusiastic. The creative urge snowed under by successive disasters was vibrantly alive once more. Chandler described what he visualized and then said he believed Wright might be able to give him what he wanted.

Still exiled from Taliesin, although friends had been trying to get a settlement with the bank, Frank went to La Jolla to work on plans for San Marcos. The following September he had a telegram, "Taliesin open for your return."

Frank knew that back of the message lay untiring effort, loyalty, and sacrifice on the part of friends who had no security except their belief in his talent, and he was deeply touched.

On the way home to Taliesin he stopped to show Dr. Chandler his design. Dr. Chandler seemed pleased but made no definite commitment. At Taliesin the house and workshop had been plundered and fields had grown up in weeds. But it was comforting to be there. Wright devoted most of his time to drawing additional plans for San Marcos and supervising apprentices who had gathered around him.

In the midst of a howling Wisconsin blizzard news came that Dr. Chandler wanted him to begin work on the San Marcos resort. Despite hazardous driving conditions Wright and several apprentices set off at once by automobile for Arizona.

In Chandler, they found that suitable quarters would cost more than they could afford to pay. Wright, who had always wanted to camp out in the region, hit upon the idea of setting up a camp for his helpers. He and the apprentices could build it if only they had a site.

The scheme appealed to Dr. Chandler, who made available a mound of splintered black rock near the land reserved for the hotel. In a cold, vacant office in Chandler Wright sat drawing a plan for the camp while shivering apprentices stood around watching and handing him necessary tools. Despite the fact that the buildings would be temporary he designed them with care, wanting them to convey the impression of having grown up out of the desert. There'd be no jerry-built construction, either. That afternoon he arranged for lumber to be delivered to the location.

Next morning after a campfire breakfast prepared at the site, Wright and the apprentices began building cabins boarded up waist high and topped by canvas. Canvas windows and doors were installed that could be opened to let in the gentle breezes or be closed against the cold. By the end of the third day quarters had been completed and cots installed for the apprentices.

Wright's own quarters, built during the next few days, fitted into the general scheme for the camp, which was named Ocatilla in honor of the scarlet blooms of that plant.

With the camp organized, Wright, established in his new drafting room where the canvas roof gave a pleasant, diffused illumination, turned to plans for Dr. Chandler's resort. There were architectural lessons to be learned from desert vegetation, he told apprentices working beside him. Look, he admonished them, at the welded, tubular construction of the cholla—and the sahuaro with interior vertical rods was a true skyscraper.

Plans for the three-hundred-room hotel shaped up into a building of concrete bricks similar to the ones used at La Miniatura, to be surrounded by terraces and pools. Because Dr. Chandler wanted to have echo organ concerts, Wright designed an organ tower of copper and block shell rising like a giant sahuaro cactus at the hotel entrance. Echo organs would be placed in adjoining hills. The dining room would be a toplit copper and glass arbor crowning the central mass.

During the hours they were not at work in the drafting room, Wright and his assistants added improvements to their camp. To connect the cabins they built a low, staggered boxboard wall with horizontal zigzags painted a dry rose color. Each cabin had a stove; and when Wright became frustrated trying to work on plans at night by gasoline light, he installed a Kohler plant.

Camp life was strenuous, but everyone enjoyed the informality of picnic-style meals and sun bathing. In the spring waxy flowers made the desert a fairyland, but as summer approached hardships increased. Rattlesnakes slithered into camp; a tarantula showed up in a clothes closet; high temperatures upped the consumption of bottled spring water that was hauled in once a week. Wright decided it would be best to break camp for the summer and return the following winter.

From Ocatilla he drove to New York to confer with Norman Guthrie, Rector at St. Mark's, concerning a nineteen-story apartment building the church intended to use as a source of revenue.

For the St. Mark's Tower Wright had planned a treelike mast structure of steel web, concrete, and glass. His drawings portrayed a building that would have strength, lightness and balance. Earthquake-proof, soundproof, it would be a novel combination of apartments and offices. The plans met with approval, but details of construction had yet to be arranged.

While Frank was in New York he had opportunity to observe current styles of architecture—as insignificant as elsewhere in the country, he concluded. The Gothic peak of the Woolworth Tower, as well as some more recent skyscrapers that looked like colonial-trimmed filing cases, struck him as monstrosities that symbolized a passion for business. Full of ornamentation, loaded with cupolas, cornices and buttresses, they were sugary and false. In the hands of architects who understood their functions they might have been proud, soaring things, but as they were they seemed only to accentuate the congestion and tumult while engulfing whole areas in darkness.

Awaiting final arrangements for St. Mark's Tower, Wright went west. On August 25, 1928, he married Olgivanna Lazovich, who, when adversity had beset him, had given proof of her loyalty and love.

Wright had met Olgivanna while attending a matinee of Russian ballet in Chicago. He had been immediately attracted to the handsome dark-haired woman with light gray eyes and aristocratic bearing. A native of Montenegro, where her family had been a distinguished one, Olgivanna spoke with an accent, but she seemed at ease whether the discussion centered on art, music, ballet or philosophy. She was an unusually intelligent woman.

Since work was to be resumed on the San Marcos plans, Wright took Olgivanna and her seven-year-old daughter, Svetlana, to Ocatilla instead of Taliesin.

That winter *Architectural Record* again published a series of his articles. In the December, 1928 issue Wright quoted Carl Sandburg, who had asked him, "Why do you use the words *poetry*, *beauty*, *truth*, or *ideal* any more? Why don't you just get down to tacks and talk about boards and nails and barn doors?"

In rebuttal Wright pointed out that poetry and truth are elemental human symbols—that poetry, rightly used, was the song, the heart of a thing and in the nature of it. Applied to architecture it was freedom of form. "Conceive, then, in love," he admonished, "and work with principle, and what men call Beauty will be the evidence of your joy in your work." *Principle* he defined as "the working scheme, the law that controls the being of anything."

Finally Wright and his apprentices completed their estimates for San Marcos. All that was lacking was Dr. Chandler's signature on the contract for construction—But before that was secured the stock market had collapsed and depression gripped the country. Instead of the forty-thousand-dollar commission he had anticipated, Frank was nineteen thousand dollars in debt on the Ocatilla Camp.

Added to this heartbreaking last-minute cancellation was a

message informing him that the depression would prevent erection of St. Mark's Tower.

Building operations across the country were virtually paralyzed. Wright wasn't sure how he'd make a living, but his heritage of independence and self-reliance left him with more defiance than despair. With Olga's understanding companionship and encouragement, Frank felt sure that, depression or no depression, he could scale new peaks of architectural achievement.

14 *CHAMPION OF YOUNG ARCHITECTS*

FOR YEARS ARCHITECTS OVERSEAS HAD BEEN CALLING WRIGHT AN architectural genius. Now his homeland was noticing him. Cornell University summoned him to speak, and in 1930 he gave a series of lectures at Princeton. One with the intriguing title, "The Cardboard House," stressed simplicity. Houses need not look like cardboard glued together in boxlike forms, said Wright, but in the past they had been too fussy and complicated. Fine architecture could not, however, be achieved merely by elimination. To know what to put in and what to leave out was to be educated in simplicity.

In a lecture entitled "Passing of the Cornice," he continued a campaign against cornices he'd been waging ever since he'd seen the collapse of the capitol in Madison. Only when the form of a thing is adapted to the function can there be superior beauty, he told his listeners. Buildings should express what they are for in the same way that the wings of an airplane express its power and purpose.

Speaking on "Style in Industry," he urged establishment of art schools where students could learn to use machines creatively and imaginatively. These schools might be connected with universities, but endowed by industries and staffed by artists in fields like textiles, woodworking, glassmaking. Machines are brainless craftsmen, Wright asserted, but they can be multipliers of manpower and when subordinated to creative intelligence can make contributions to architecture.

Each successive lecture brought out larger audiences. A dramatist by nature, Wright had a pleasing platform manner. His voice was mellow, his smile disarming, haunting. The twinkle in his light gray eyes when he was relating a humorous incident could be replaced the next moment by flashing scorn as with denunciatory zeal he flayed shoddy construction.

In his lecture "Machinery, Materials, and Men" he stressed the idea that the inappropriate cannot be beautiful. The beauty of wood lies in its quality as wood. Staining wood, for example, may retain its character, or even heighten the beauty of its wavelike contours, but painting destroys delicate nuances of color and markings. Imitations torture and degrade.

On the subject "Tyranny of the Skyscraper" Wright contended that skyscrapers had been built not for the benefit of humanity but for the profit of their proprietors.

Following the Princeton lectures Wright appeared in Seattle, Denver, Minneapolis, Chicago, Milwaukee. Everywhere he found young people eager, enthusiastic, and ready with questions.

About this time Wright got an invitation from the Pan American Union to go to Rio de Janeiro as a member of a jury representing North America to judge drawings submitted in a worldwide competition for a memorial to Columbus. Since the invitation included his wife Olga, Frank was delighted to have her at his side.

In October of 1930 they boarded a vessel that was half freighter. One of the interesting persons aboard was Finnish architect Eero Saarinen. By the time the boat nosed into the harbor at Rio the two men had become good friends.

When the boat landed, boys swarmed over it clamoring for Wright. They introduced themselves as students at the Brazilian Belles Artes and explained that they were out on strike because their professors had banned the reading of Wright's books. Would he plead their cause?

"Look out," Saarinen warned. "This is a revolutionary country —first thing you know, *sskk*." He drew a finger across his throat.

Wright, now sixty-one but vigorous physically and mentally, promised to help. Seeking out Herbert Moses, editor of *El Globo*, he converted him to his point of view. Later Wright met with his opponents in the old hall of the Belles Artes. On the stage sat faculty representatives, Ambassador Morgan, and the handsome president of the University of Brazil, who presided at the meeting. Wright knew less Portuguese than the president knew English, but Moses from *El Globo* was on hand to translate.

In the audience there were perhaps seven hundred students. After Latinesque formalities had been disposed of, Wright spoke in behalf of the strikers. At the end of the meeting students charged the judges' bench, pushed dignitaries aside, picked Wright up and carried him out to a taxi. Then with all hanging aboard who could stick on, they rode off to the hotel Copacabana, where the Wrights were staying.

Carrying a torch for the Belles Artes boys, Frank wrote newspaper articles and spoke innumerable times at dinners and meetings. Everywhere he went, flashes announced the presence of reporters or camera fans taking pictures. As far as Wright was concerned judging for the Columbus memorial took a back seat, but he concurred when ballots were cast for a young Englishman to receive the award.

When the National Academy in Brazil tendered Wright an honorary membership, he accepted on condition that the society help the students at the Belles Artes in their struggle for freedom. He made the same proposition when the Architects Society of Brazil extended honorary membership. Both groups assented. After one of the professors who had been speaking alongside Wright was arrested, Saarinen told him, "Your turn next."

Conscious of the fact that Rio de Janeiroans resented the use of "America" in speaking of the United States, Frank began using the word Usonian. This was a term coined by Samuel Butler, author of *Erewhon*. "American," Butler had said, belonged to South American countries as well as North American—hence Usonian, derived from the root "union."

Wright and Olga, simply dressed but looking like the patrician she was, spent a weekend at Petropolis, swam and sunbathed on the beach in front of the Copacabana, went sightseeing and visited the steamer *Atlantique*. They became very fond of the emotional

Latins who entertained them lavishly. On the last night of their six weeks' stay in Rio, students in native costume, playing improvised instruments, serenaded them at the Copacabana.

The trip home was a leisurely one. Back at Taliesin Frank was much in demand as a public speaker. Frequently there was a request for an exhibition of his works in connection with a lecture. In 1931 he spoke at the Chicago Art Institute on "The Young Man In Architecture". He warned that young men should not go into the profession for money, but for love of the work. Would-be architects, he said, should take plenty of time to prepare, and should study machines—their processes, purposes, products. They should analyze the details in buildings, not for the purpose of imitation, but for the discovery of principle.

"To get into the practice half baked," he told his listeners, "is to sell out your birthright as an architect for a mess of pottage."

He advised that, once in practice, architects should think of quality whether building a chicken coop or a cathedral. "Don't be afraid to be yourselves," he admonished. "Being thought ridiculous is preferable to being cowardly." Young men, he believed, should be shock troops thrown into action against corruption of the American ideal.

"Keep your own ideal of honesty so high that your dearest ambition in life will be to call yourself an honest man, and look yourself in the face," he told his audience.

One afternoon while Wright was in the gallery at the Chicago Art Institute where he had an exhibit, a tall, handsome woman came toward him. Her manner was friendly, but for a moment he did not recognize her.

"Catherine!" he exclaimed.

As they went around viewing the exhibit together, Catherine, who had remarried, assured him she was perfectly happy.

Traveling from place to place giving lectures heightened Frank's distaste for urbanization. In *The Disappearing City*, published in 1932, he wrote that cities had once been a necessity from the standpoint of defense and convenience, but now ease of communication, electrification, mechanical heating and refrigeration had made dispersal possible. Cities, he argued, had become volcanic craters of confused forces, unfit places in which to work, because individuals crowded into unhealthy, artificially-lighted, densely-packed cells were surrounded by congestion, confusion, and a bedlam of harsh noises. Here they became pullers of levers, pressers of buttons. Slaves of the herd instinct, they were lost as human beings.

Wright pictured the city as a menace to the future of humanity, because citizens buffeted by the continual motion to and fro would become incapable of meditation and lose sight of the true aim of existence. America, he said, must pioneer in decentralization.

As the nineteen thirties plunged the country into deeper depression, Wright had more opportunity to state his architectural philosophy than to practice it. Repeatedly he was frustrated, drawing plans that failed to come to completion. One day a new thought occurred to him. If he couldn't build buildings, why not not build the builders of buildings?

To Olga he outlined a scheme for a fellowship of apprentices in which there would be an attempt to integrate architecture with other arts and industrial processes. There would be no formal courses, classes, or lectures, but students would learn by doing through work experiences at Taliesin and also in Wright's building projects. Young men upon leaving would have no degree, but would have a testimonial of fitness to practice architecture.

"How many apprentices and where would you house them?" questioned Olga.

Wright first said seventy, but then reduced the number to twenty-three. As for housing, the old Hillside Home School buildings at a convenient distance from the house would serve admirably. Their untended desolation had been disturbing him for some time.

To begin with, Wright would be the faculty; later he'd bring in a painter, a musician and a sculptor. The Fellowship would be as much a way of life as a course in architecture, with each apprentice developing into a well-integrated individual. So that the group would be welded into a true fellowship, Wright planned that tasks connected with communal living and maintenance of Taliesin should be accomplished through division of labor.

For apprentices Wright did not want one-sided specialists. He preferred young men with stamina who would be equipped to work manually as well as intellectually. Together he and Olga prepared and sent out a circular letter to a small list of friends. In it they described Fellowship goals and the accommodations. The fee for a full year would be six hundred and fifty dollars.

To get the Hillside Home buildings ready for the Fellowship, Wright rounded up a labor force of unemployed men who, because of the depression, were willing to work for little more than room and board. The men were housed in the old Hillside School laundry, which Olga tried to make cheerful and comfortable.

Unperturbed by the responsibilities he had assumed, Wright went on carefree excursions with the family. One September morning in 1932 all of them walked barefooted over the hills, while their German shepherd Kave leaped beside them. In a garden patch below the reservoir they broke open a ripe melon to eat. Frank enjoyed the pink sweetness as much as the children— Svetlana now had a younger sister Iovanna.

By the time sumac was scarlet and acorns dropped from flaming oaks, twenty-three apprentices had arrived. Each was assigned a room which he could decorate in any way he wished.

At the first meeting of the group Wright explained that the Fellowship would be a student body, a farm labor force, and a construction crew. The few women students and wives of apprentices could weave or pursue artistic interests. Learning to work together was important. A poet or painter might create masterpieces in seclusion, but the architect must always cooperate with others.

Almost immediately Wright assigned problems in the drafting room. As students settled down to intense, quiet concentration, he saw in each one a potential artist yearning for realization. Momentarily a question assailed him. How could he teach without dogma, how keep apprentices from slavish imitation?

Under the guidance of Charlie Curtis, a seventy-nine-year-old

Cornish mason, the boys learned how to chip stones and fit walls together. "You've got to get the feel o' the rocks in your hands m' boys," he would tell them in a kindly way. "It hain't no use 'til y' do. No use 't all."

Will Schwanke, a sure-handed Spring Green carpenter, oversaw carpentry construction, of which there was an abundance with Hillside buildings being remodeled for Fellowship purposes. Most of the apprentices found the learn-by-doing approach very efficient, but a few who had been accustomed to rote learning and lectures were disturbed by the informality of Wright's techniques. Rather than lay down formal rules he taught by example, showing them the effect of one texture or form against another, giving them appreciation of shape, form, line. This instruction went on not just in the drafting room or on a work project, but hourly, even at the dinner table in informal discussion.

Students not used to manual labor were, at first, unhappy at Taliesin. One of these who did not share Wright's concept that *all* work is important, and who was of the opinion that he was qualified to handle a drawing pencil but not a saw, was excused from menial chores. Later, tired of being ribbed, and feeling guilty over his parasitism, he volunteered to carry his part of the load.

Not all assigned tasks were physical. Because Wright thought architects should be articulate, he encouraged apprentices to take turns writing articles for the *Capitol Times* and the *State Journal* in Madison. Occasionally he himself wrote one.

The Fellowship hit a snag when they badly needed more lumber and Wright could not afford the price lumberyards were asking. After a lot of scouting around he located four hundred acres of virgin oak from which he could take out trees. With the help of several farmers and a caterpillar tractor, apprentices turned loggers. The lumber was green and sometimes crookedly sawed, but they used it anyway.

Apprentices worked hard, beginning their day at six thirty, but they also had plenty of opportunity for recreation. Snowy hills and ice-locked streams afforded facilities for coasting and ice skating.

Special holidays were occasions for festivity and surprises. On

Halloween there was a masked ball. For informal get-togethers the Fellowship had its own living room, previously the assembly room for Hillside, where quotations from Isaiah had been carved in oak beams and verses from Gray's "Elegy" in the sandstone over the fireplace.

Frequently apprentices settled themselves around a huge fireplace in Wright's quarters for an informal discussion of architecture. With a dreamy expression on his furrowed, bronzed face Wright would share with them his feeling about the architectural quality in music—the sense of design. Beethoven, he showed them, built an edifice of sound to which, like a good architect, he added nothing that was superfluous or merely pretty.

The gymnasium of Hillside School was being converted into a theater where the Fellowship saw movies, gave concerts and staged plays. Olga, versatile but unobtrusive, was clever in dredging up talent. A shy boy might be brought out through masking him and giving him a dashing part in a play. Another she would teach to play piano, or to dance.

Wright's investment in the builders of buildings gave him great satisfaction as he watched apprentices develop into architects and individuals.

15 *WRIGHT VERSUS BOXMENT*

WRIGHT WAS WARM AND RESPONSIVE TOWARD HIS APPRENTICES, but did not let the Fellowship deprive him of time for the children, with whom he often played imaginative games. Curly-haired Iovanna asked endless questions like, "Will you buy me some flying wings at Marshall Field's so I can fly up into the sky to see God?"

Often the family read together. Watching Svetlana's reactions to a story, Wright would think she was the embodiment of her name, which meant "light" in Russian. The children and Olga were bringing him more contentment than he'd ever known.

When spring came apprentices began each day by working an hour in the garden. Afterwards some went to the drafting room, some planted trees; others checked the electric fence, hauled gravel and graded roads. For the chores in fields or on buildings Wright named a head man for a fortnight, and he in turn assigned tasks to assistants.

As problems arose Wright dealt with them ingeniously. Defeated in attempts to buy badly needed lime at a price he could afford, he tracked down the owner of an old lime kiln and got permission to fix it up. Then he brought in an elderly lime burner to teach the apprentices how to use it.

Confronted by the necessity for keeping the fire going continuously, boys ate their meals beside the kiln. Nights when the flames lighted up the countryside Wright would see apprentices stripped to their shorts like stokers in the hold of a ship as they took their turn tending the fire.

By summer it was evident that the Fellowship was destined to be a success. But Wright had underestimated expenses. Wanting to feed the apprentices well, he supervised the marketing and would load down the old Auburn Cord with boxes, bags, crates of fruit and sacks of flour until it looked like a beast of burden. Tea was served at four o'clock, and for between-meal snacks there were bowls of grapes, apples, peanuts and hickory nuts. Under Olgivanna's direction the food was well prepared—but the cost was alarming.

One obvious solution was to raise the tuition, but money was scarce everywhere. If fees went up could talented young men afford to come to Taliesin?

While making plans for the Fellowship, Wright, influenced by Olgivanna, had also written an account of his life and experiences in architecture. Titled *An Autobiography* it had been released early in 1932. Although the book had little unity or chronology it was written with beauty, sensitivity, and vividness. Bits of humor enlivened it, as well as candid accounts of his own errors in judgment. One of these had to do with the Imperial Hotel. Japanese consultants had advised making a protective cover shed with a tight roof and sides of matting, but to Wright that had seemed an unwarranted expense. Now he estimated that had the precaution been taken the Imperial could have been completed seven months sooner with greater comfort for all concerned.

The details, sometimes belligerent, of Wright's struggles against conservatism, conformity, and ignorance lend courage to all who want to stand for principles regardless of opposition.

By means of articles and lectures Wright had much to say about the International School of Architecture—so called because its practitioners believed industrial techniques and the new scientific approach were fundamentally international in character and that architecture, if adapted to the world of machines, must also be international. A leader in this line of thought was Walter Gropius, who had founded the Bauhaus.

Extremists of the International School insisted that function was all-important, even at the expense of proportion, balance, rhythm, or harmonious relation to site. The argument that form should be derived from function had been advanced by Wright years before. His experimentation up to 1910, his Wasmuth-published monograph and exhibits had greatly influenced some of those now allying themselves with the International School. It looked to him, he said, as if organic architecture having gone abroad had come back turned edgewise, minus beauty. Yet beauty was as real a function as convenience.

Wright disagreed violently with Parisian Le Corbusier, who since the nineteen twenties had been calling for a modern architecture that would shed excessive ornament. A house, Corbusier had said, was a machine for living.

In this Wright sensed a distressing lack of individuality. Machines should build the building, he believed, but the building itself need not be a machine. And in his opinion the proper use of ornament could embellish practical needs. Buildings completely devoid of it looked stark and naked.

Wright was not one to temper his remarks. Sometimes at a banquet or a dinner Olgivanna would have a warning frown on her sensitive brow as he launched into an attack on architects who dealt in "boxment à la mode" or who "in a craze of verticality, advocated tall, taller, tallest." Often he perversely ignored his wife.

Sometimes Wright's biting statements spurred the self-contented to higher achievement, but unfortunately they occasionally hurt architects who were both honest and serious. Despite the fact that he characterized the use of columns, cornices and other classical features as "neurotic nostalgia," there were some who believed works of the past could provide guiding principles. While Wright was haranguing other architects they were retaliating by calling his work crack-brained, impractical and expensive.

When Wright heard about plans for the International Exposition of 1933 to be held in Chicago, he objected to the plans for false buildings and pretentious scenes. He was not invited to participate on the steering committee, nor was his name on the roster for exhibits. The reason given was that he would seek to dominate. At a special meeting of The American Union of

Decorative Artists and Craftsmen, the members protested his non-employment, but nothing came of their action.

The 1893 Fair had imposed classicism; the 1933 one imposed a false modernism, but Wright was too involved with the Fellowship to pay much attention. During the preceding winter, a severe one, he had spent thirty-five hundred dollars on fuel. At times it had seemed as if half the apprentices spent all their time and energy chopping and hauling wood to keep the other half warm. Prospects of a similar fuel bill plus the task of maintaining harmony among apprentices cooped up during cold spells dismayed him. If only the Fellowship could be shifted to a region where they could be outdoors and build all winter long. His thoughts traveled back to the Ocatilla Camp, where he'd fallen in love with the incomparably pure air and blue sky, the vastness, and the unforgettable amalgam of scents.

"What would you think of moving the Fellowship to Arizona for the winter?" he asked Olga.

In November a little caravan of cars and trucks loaded with sleeping bags and other camp equipment rolled toward Dr. Chandler's hacienda at Chandler, Arizona. Wright's goal was to build a camp similar to Ocatilla, which had been carried away by Indians; but first he had to find a site.

When the desert came into view he was charmed all over again by the vistas. Like nomads, the Fellowship roamed across the desert seeking a location for a permanent camp.

"We must study nature," Wright told the roving apprentices; "it can reveal principles, form, design, the inner rhythm of all being." He told them of a Welsh triad: "A genius is a man who has an eye to see nature, a man with a heart to feel nature, a man with the boldness to follow nature."

From nature an architect could learn lessons about the use of ornament. Nature never sticks an ornament on—it is always *of* the thing. On the other hand, Wright cautioned, plainness is not necessarily grace or beauty, and simplicity is not the side of a barn.

Frank did not find a suitable location for the camp, and in May the Fellowship headed for Wisconsin to plant gardens and fields.

Complications awaited them. Although the depression had become more severe, prices on building supplies had not been reduced. There was also a shortage of manpower, because workmen who had been doing odd jobs at Taliesin had gone on relief, preferring to be paid for idleness. During Wright's absence, labor agitators had stirred up discontent. But when apprentices took over on jobs previously doled out to local labor, some men who wanted jobs and weren't hired made ugly threats.

As labor troubles subsided, Wright gave much thought to urban planning. The drift toward cities had been senseless and unthinking. They had become prison houses of the soul, Wright believed, with nothing to distinguish number 337611 from 337610. Writing on *The City of Tomorrow* in *Pictorial Review*, March 1933, he stated that the skyscraper was an example of extremity in the wrong direction and that cities had ceased to answer human needs.

Wright was not the only architect to raise his voice against the irrational growth of centers of population. In a pamphlet titled *Urbanisme*, Le Corbusier had written that towns were ineffectual, "using up bodies and threatening souls."

To make more tangible his own lofty ideas about what cities should be like, Wright, with the help of his apprentices, launched a decentralization project he called Broadacre City. On a large relief map representing a four-square-mile area, they placed elaborate built-to-scale models of houses, farms, factories and schools.

A mixture of rural and urban elements, Broadacre was planned for the needs of eighteen hundred persons. Farms, flowers and fields rubbed elbows with the city hall. Service stations were to become distributing centers for merchandise, and also provide adequate parking and overnight accommodations. There would be roadside markets with fresh produce. Concave highways would be free of archaic telephone poles and glaring billboards. Businessmen would have offices connected with their residences; factory employees would be within walking distance of their plant.

The farm experiences of his boyhood had given Frank a love for space and growing things. In Broadacre, land was not divided up piecemeal into fifty-foot lots. Each family had at least an acre of property. In such a vernal countryside, with privacy and beauty for everyone, people could escape the pressure of city life.

Instead of houses built parallel to streets, so that they would of necessity have one bright side and one dark side, each house would be placed so that the sun would shine in every room part of each day. Intended to show machine-age luxury at its best, one of the models in the Broadacre project was House on the Mesa. Its spread-out cubes were planned for a five-car family.

Even Wright conceded that cities like Broadacre could come only gradually. To make it a reality there would have to be freedom from land speculation, planned distribution centers, controls over individuals who might otherwise deface the community. But Wright hoped his model would lead to new efficiency in city planning. In 1935 Broadacre was exhibited at Rockefeller Center.

That same year Wright visited the Bad Lands and Black Hills of South Dakota. The coloring of the sculptured masses of the Bad Lands left him in awe of their unusual architecture. At Mount Rushmore in the Black Hills he was much interested in the gigantic face of Washington emerging from the rock on the side of a canyon under the direction of sculptor Gutzon Borglum. Frank returned to Taliesin refreshed by the beauty he had seen—gemlike Sylvan Lake, pine-blanketed hills, rock-ribbed Spearfish Canyon.

There seemed to be no let-up in the depression, and by 1936 Frank's financial obligations began to look insurmountable. To his rescue came Philadelphian Edgar Kaufmann with a request for a house to be built at Bear Run, Pennsylvania. Wright always wanted to relate his houses to earth, soil and climate. Was the site hilly, flat, sunshiny, shady? What kind of rocks, trees, birds surrounded it? What special virtues or faults did it have?

As soon as Kaufmann mentioned a waterfall and his delight in the tinkle and rush of it, Wright immediately put it mentally into his plans. Upon inspection he found the property was in an area forested by oaks and maples. Beside the waterfall rose a solid rock ledge. Wright's idea for the dwelling was wild and poetic—a house with the front part cantilevered over the waterfall and the rear fitted into the rock ledge.

"Falling Water," Bear Run, Pennsylvania

The completed design for Falling Water appealed to Kaufmann. He objected, however, when Wright brought in apprentices to help with the planning, arguing that they would make costly mistakes. Only after Frank pointed out the necessity for providing opportunities for developing young architects did Kaufmann assent. Their enthusiasm, intelligence, and faithful cooperation won him over. Actually they added little to expenses, because they knew what Wright wanted.

Built of reinforced concrete that harmonized with the stone ledges, Falling Water was a fantasy of cantilevers on cantilevers collected on struts that wedded the house to the cliffside. Its lines were rhythmic and powerful. The main story consisted almost entirely of one great room opening into subordinate spaces. On the upper floor individual suites opened on private terraces. The rear of the house was solid, but the front was a series of glass frames with glazed stairs leading from the living room down to the pool.

When the moment arrived to pull down the last bit of scaffolding from which the cantilevered terrace had been cast, workmen refused to carry out the job, fearing that the house would collapse and bury them in the ruins. Seizing an ax, Wright removed the support himself. The house, a masterpiece of construction, seemed to float in space.

16 CONTROVERSY OVER PILLARS AND HEXAGONS

IN JULY OF 1936 HERBERT JOHNSON OF THE S. C. JOHNSON WAX Company came to Taliesin accompanied by publicity man Jack Lewis. The firm, Johnson told Wright, wanted a modern office building that would be convenient yet beautiful, an inspiring place in which to work.

Wright designed a brick, steel-reinforced building that would be fireproof, earthquake-proof, soundproof, air-conditioned, floor-heated. As the planning progressed he added new features— a carport, squash courts, and a hemicycle wired for sound that could seat two hundred and fifty and could be used for lectures or movies to entertain the employees.

As contractor for the Johnson Administration Building, Wright was fortunate in having Ben Wiltsheck, a student of architecture and a careful builder. The two men had confidence in each other. Wiltsheck was also skillful in organizing the varied activities on the site, from the pouring of concrete to the installation of fixtures.

For any building Wright always performed many tests—tests on cantilevers, stairs, or concrete—tests to determine strength, lightness and efficiency. Because of the unconventionality of his techniques he frequently had become involved in altercations with enforcers of building codes. Uniform rules were a necessity, he realized, but often a hindrance, because they were unimaginative or outworn. Codes got in Wright's way once more on the Johnson Building. His plan called for an office studded with slender, tapered, almost flowerlike columns with cores of cold-drawn steel mesh reinforcements in which a membrane of steel would become one with the concrete. By having the concrete agitated during pouring, he knew it would be possible to strengthen the columns even more. That they could bear more weight than ever would be placed upon them Wright was absolutely certain, but when he turned his plans over to the Wisconsin Building Commission, the members were aghast. According to their rule-of-thumb formula for measuring stress these "flimsy" columns would not support the required load.

Furthermore the code allowed a maximum height of only six feet for columns nine inches in diameter. Frank's were twenty-four feet high. What the commissioners seemed not to realize was that besides a vivid imagination Wright had an intuitive, almost infallible knowledge of materials and engineering.

The commission refused to grant a building permit unless the nine-inch columns were changed to ones three feet in diameter. These would have been clumsy, ugly, and space robbing. Frank appealed to Johnson, who appeared with him before the commission to ask permission to conduct a test. In a field Wright set up a duplicate of the type of column to be used and steadied it by means of diagonal wooden braces. A platform topped it.

On the hour and day appointed, Wright, accompanied by "Hib" Johnson and several Taliesin apprentices, met the commissioners. Despite the cold so many reporters and curious bystanders turned out that the police had to rope off the area.

Workmen, using a crane, deposited weighed amounts of pig iron, gravel, sand, and cement in large bags on the platform. Wright, with the usual pork-pie hat atop his cloud of silver hair, and a shawl around his shoulders, superintended. To meet requirements the pillar would have to support twelve tons.

The crane kept swinging and dumping. At twelve tons there was no indication of stress. As the load became double what the column would ever have to carry and the pillar showed no sign of collapse, an impish twinkle appeared in Wright's eyes.

Afternoon waned but the crane continued. Thirty tons, forty, fifty. By nightfall the weight had reached sixty. There was no more room to pile on any more bags. The commissioners disappeared

Johnson's Wax Buildings, Racine, Wisconsin

without a word. Examination showed that the platform had cracked but the shaft was unbroken.

"Not only safe but unpredictably strong," Hib Johnson told reporters.

Wright got the building permit.

Where was the secret, architects and engineers asked afterward.

"In curving expansion," Wright told them. The stresses had been planned to be diagonal rather than right-angled.

As the building progressed, the Taliesin Fellowship helped with details. By this time the public was asking questions about Wright's training methods for young architects.

In an article on "Apprenticeship Training" written for the *Architectural Record*, September 1936, he stated that in his estimation formal school education played only a small part in the making of an architect. What was needed, he believed, was experience in learning the nature of materials, in working with them, in planning and building. Young architects should have inspired leadership.

Apprentices at Taliesin had many opportunities to learn the nature of materials. Wright, who liked the feeling of stone under his fingers, who saw the gold glinting in the grain of wood, and the clay of brick like colors on a palette, conveyed his sensitivity to his students. Every material had its own message, its own lyrical song, he told them. To utter any language you must know the alphabet, and the alphabet for the machine age was the nature and appropriate use of steel, glass and concrete.

Wright also gave his apprentices the inspired leadership he'd said was a requisite. "Modern architecture is young architecture," he asserted. "The joy of youth must develop it." Without joy in work there could be no true creativity. Humanity best loved work with some gaiety in it.

There were as many paths toward success, he challenged them, as there were architects with capacity for taking infinite pains.

Now more young men were clamoring to become apprentices than Wright could accommodate. They came because they had read his books or seen his buildings or had heard about him and wanted to learn his secrets. Some of them hitchhiked to Taliesin.

Wright had no standard questionnaire for applicants, but enthusiasm was a vital necessity.

Next to spirit, character counted most. He wanted young men who were honest and responsible and who would give voluntary apprenticeship, not discipleship. To aspirants for the Fellowship he put such questions as, "Know anything about drafting? Are you willing to learn by doing? What are your goals?" He was not interested in those who courted popular acclaim, or who concentrated too much on winning a point for their own personal glory. Becoming involved in selfish pursuits made one's art suffer, he believed. An architect should seek to be of service to his times. It was no good to get the tools of a creative artist unless you used them for humanity.

Youths who displayed something touching or fine in the course of an interview were accepted even if they couldn't pay the fee, which had been raised to eleven hundred dollars a year.

The quality of an apprentice was brought to light during the trial period of three months. At Taliesin recreation was encouraged, but not inactivity. A few novices, brilliant but coddled, found the routines exhausting and tumbled into bed at night worn out. Some who came were ill-prepared to cope with communal life and did not blend into the Fellowship, where presumption or pretence was quickly uncovered. To those unaccustomed to interior discipline, Wright pointed out that there is no discipline so severe as the discipline of a great ideal, but no discipline yields such rich rewards. Since law and order are the basis of beauty, there can be no lawlessness in architecture.

Individuality was indispensable, but egotism he called a sickly disease of consciousness. The few who were slackers, incompetents, malcontents, or bigots were weeded out. The aggressive, bad-mannered, or hot-tempered learned better or were eliminated.

Most of the apprentices were starry-eyed, dedicated young men who pursued architecture like a religion. One of Wright's favorites was tall, dark-eyed Wesley Peters. Alert and energetic, Wes was loyal to Taliesin and its ideals. With a natural capacity for leadership he served as a right-hand man for Frank. When Svetlana and Wes, who had been attracted to one another from their first meeting, left Taliesin in pursuit of education and career interests, Frank felt bereft.

In addition to their duties in connection with an ever-expanding Taliesin, apprentices now cultivated two hundred acres of farmland, filled the root cellar with vegetables grown in the garden, preserved fruits, and made wine from hillside grapes. Wright supervised the care of chickens, Holsteins, horses, geese and peacocks, sharing the life of constructive action. Nothing about him indicated age except his white hair.

By 1937 Taliesin had a U-shape with a master wing on one side, apprentice rooms on the other, plus workrooms, kitchen and dining halls. Each apprentice's room with natural-colored woods and bright walls had built-in furniture, shelves, a drawing board, and a fireplace.

As they went about their daily activities members of the Fellowship were drenched with music. A loudspeaker in a tower overlooking the hill garden poured out oratorios, concertos and symphonies. From the Wrights' living quarters often came the sound of a piano or the tinkle of a harpsichord. The harpsichord had been bought at a time when funds had been low and the temperature in Taliesin almost freezing because of lack of fuel. When a commission had come along unexpectedly, Wright bought the musical instrument instead of coal. Strains of violin or cello played by apprentices issued from studios. In almost every room in the main part of Taliesin there was a piano—even on a tiny balcony in the drafting room.

In the theater built in the old gym of the Hillside School, seats made by the apprentices were placed at angles to the screen and circled upward in tiers in such a way that the audience had almost a face-to-face relationship with the actors. Roofs and walls were oak. Over the huge studio windows, left open on summer nights, were roll-up bamboo-like shades.

The stage was completely recessed, but the movie screen stood free like an easel undraped and unframed. Loudspeakers beneath the stage pointed toward the rear wall. Camera equipment was in the balcony. Stage curtains, craft work of the Fellowship, were brilliant-colored felt abstractions applied to neutral coarse cotton fabric. Here once a week or oftener the Fellowship assembled for a play, a concert, or movies. Wright's enjoyment of films, especially ones having to do with travel, was uninhibited and complete.

In the summer and fall when weather permitted, the Fellowship swam, rode horseback, and went on picnics, sometimes combined with fruit picking or gathering of hickory nuts or black walnuts. At least once a week a fleet of Indian-red cars and trucks would roll out over the hills to a suitable spot for a campfire. While salting a hamburger or supervising a broiled steak, Wright would make observations on the flora, fauna, and geology of the region.

Sunday night was a dressy occasion. Olgivanna had felt that once a week the Fellowship should have the appearance of ladies and gentlemen. Girls wore evening gowns and dinner was served on trays in the theater or in the Wrights' lavishly carpeted living room with its tawny gold plaster. To bring outdoor touches to the indoors for these occasions, apprentices helped make lifelike arrangements of weeds, seasonal flowers or bittersweet to blend with pre-Ming pottery, Japanese prints, Indian baskets, blue Chinese porcelain, Persian tiles and Scandinavian pewter.

Usually there was a program after dinner on Sunday night. Reflecting Wright's insistence on the full, rounded life, Taliesin boasted a choir, chamber music groups, and a recorder group for which Svetlana had worked up interest. Iovanna played harp and Olga showed professional prowess as a pianist. The apprentices liked to sing informally and a favorite was the "T-Square and Triangle Work Song," verses for which Wright had composed years before and Olgivanna, with a flair for composition, had set to music.

After the program Wright, regally flanked by Olgivanna seated amid a luxurious assortment of fur rugs and cushions, might read aloud, charm his listeners with his lively gift of narrative, or discourse with inexhaustible eloquence on Japanese art, economics, cultural lag, religion, or philosophy.

"Great architecture is based on universal, eternal principles," he told them, whether the edifice be built by Mayans or men on Mars. Unless architectural values are human values, they are not valuable. "Find new applications of power to purpose," Wright advised. He urged apprentices to dramatize not the machine but man.

Frequently, distinguished guests were at Taliesin on Sunday night to speak to the Fellowship and share in the lofty but spirited conversation.

Monday morning the apprentices would resume their practical duties with renewed enthusiasm. Despite continuation of the depression Wright was getting commissions. The world seemed finally to be content to let him live his own life and to work in his own way.

Early in 1937 he was at work on a house for Paul R. Hanna, Associate Professor of Education at Stanford University. Three years prior to this the Hannas had come to Wright to discuss plans for a house at Palo Alto with plenty of view and space. A person interested in education and books should not live in the same kind of house as one interested in dramatics, business, or engines, thought Wright, mulling over a design that would best meet the needs of the Hannas. As usual he asked himself what materials were available in the Palo Alto region, what labor would be available? Would manual or machine labor be best, or both?

Because of Hanna's modest salary, a luxury house was not a possibility. Since 1927 Gropius had been experimenting with economical, functional, factory-made houses. Wright was not at all in sympathy with Gropius' ideal of evolving a perfect design and then manufacturing replicas—unless individualized, such houses would be stupid make-shifts—but he had no objections to using prefabricated materials. For the Hanna house he decided to use plywood but have the house built by hand.

And why not make the dwelling hexagonal in shape? The hexagon was rhythmic and would stimulate imagination. Since the house and rooms in it would have obtuse corners, as in a honeycomb, the Hannas christened it Honeycomb House.

Early spring rains in 1937 retarded progress, and as the building proceeded, labor costs mounted. Besides that, Wright and the Hannas were not in agreement on furnishings for Honeycomb House. This was not unusual. Frank believed a house should be an harmonious whole, with the architect planning the house inside

Hanna House, Palo Alto, California

and outside. Almost resentful of intrusion by the client, he would, if left to himself, work out everything to minute details such as having a craftsman weave hangings with gold threads to echo copper accessories.

Many clients wanted to bring in a decorator to help with interiors, but Wright, who called them "inferior decorators," maintained they were enemies of organic architecture and that they overcrowded interiors, making them look like overdressed women. The problem with the Hannas was that he wanted them to discard all their old furniture and let him design hexagonal furniture to go with the house. In the end the Hannas consented, and chairs, ottomans and tables were all hexagon-shaped.

Visitors to Honeycomb House admired the glass walls facing the hills and built in such a way that they could be rolled back on warm days. Trees, flowers, the fog rolling in all seemed like part of the house. But critics wondered if Wright hadn't been striving for the merely novel effect of a peculiar shape. To some the results seemed harsh and forced.

Wright's reward came when the Hannas reported that living there had resulted in a lessening of tension. They said that the shape gave a greater sense of space, of serenity. To Wright a building, as truly as a poem or concerto, should be an outpouring of the heart. Only heart-built houses could enrich the lives of those who lived in them. He was gratified when the Hannas said that they felt the new home would leave an imprint on the characters of their three children, cultivating in them beauty as a way of living.

17 *USONIAN HOUSES, A CAMP, AND A CAMPUS*

BEFORE THE JOHNSON ADMINISTRATION BUILDING WAS COMPLETED, young Hib Johnson, impressed by the way the structure was progressing, came to Wright to discuss plans for a house at Wind Point, north of Racine, Wisconsin. His site was a forty-acre tract of land on the shore of Lake Michigan. The house was for his bride.

After Hib had gone, Wright let the building take form in imagination first. Only after an idea lived should it be put on paper. The purpose of T-square and triangle should be to modify, elaborate on, or test a conception. Because the house was designed with four wings it would be named Wingspread. The outside walls were to be of cypress plank and brick veneer, the roof of tile. Surrounding it would be collateral gardens and a pool for wild fowl.

When the house was three-fourths finished the bride died and Hib lost all interest in the completion of Wingspread. Both as architect and friend Frank tried to persuade him not to leave the house an empty shell. His wife would have wanted him to finish what had been begun so happily, and he needed the house as a retreat for himself and two sons by a previous marriage.

Finally Hib had it finished with every detail as he and his wife had planned it, even to the abstract wings of cast bronze on a door plate set in the inside stone slab of the doorsill to signify the name Wingspread. Frank was gratified when he saw the soothing effect the house had on Hib. Both were pleased at the way it enhanced the view. For no reason that he could explain, Wright felt that Wingspread would be the last of his prairie houses.

When he received an invitation from the Soviet Union to attend a world conference of architects in Moscow and travel in Russia as an honored guest, he accepted eagerly, having long wanted to see that country and explore its political philosophy. In May of 1937 he and Olga disembarked from the *Queen Mary* at Cherbourg. After a short stop in Paris they went on to Berlin and then to Russia.

At the border—a wide, blank space minus trees but bristling with barbed wire entanglements and sentry-manned towers— there was a long-drawn-out examination of luggage. After cross-questioning, the Wrights took a train to Moscow. Olgivanna, who had been Russian-educated, acted as interpreter. Frank thought the Kremlin beautiful, and the Moscow subway made New York's seem like a sewer, but he found most of the buildings hard, coarse and badly proportioned. Marble columns and glistening chandeliers had been overused, and the Work Palace suffered from a striving for grand effects that hadn't come off.

Attending the meetings of the World Institute of Architects, Frank was delighted by the comradeship, solidarity, and idealism. With some of the young Russian architects he felt a real kinship. When he appeared to speak to the Institute and guests meeting in the Hall of Soviets, where so many purge trials had been held, the audience gave him a standing ovation.

The Wrights visited a number of Russian cities. Deep in the country Frank was surprised to find the trees and flowers much the same as at Taliesin. A great road-making program was under way and near Leningrad young girls with white kerchiefs over their hair were driving steam rollers. To make way for erection of buildings old churches and other buildings were being dynamited.

Everywhere the Wrights went they were most hospitably received. All expenses were paid by the government—even laundry and telegrams. Russia appeared to be a land of opportunity. On the streets individuals spoke proudly of "our" theater, "our" museum.

Upon his return to America, Wright said he felt the United

States was not hearing the truth about the USSR. This led to charges that he was a Communist. Actually, although he admired the energy and spirit of the Russian people and was excited over some of their experiments, he was an ardent supporter of democracy.

Back at Taliesin, Wright entered zestfully into activities there. In the drafting room a word that came often to his lips was *integral*. "Nothing is of value except as it is naturally related to the whole in the direction of some living purpose," he told the apprentices.

For some time Wright had been saying to anyone who would listen that America's major architectural problem had become building, at a moderate cost, houses that would still have artistic excellence and originality. The kind of house he visualized he called Usonian. Usonia, he quipped, meant the United States as it should be. These dwellings must have a harmonious relationship to their environment, but must also be for the life lived in the building.

Architects of the International School drew a sharp line between man and nature and between house and land, often stressing contrasts, but Wright adhered to his old theory that buildings should be organic—always of the land.

On the subject of interiors Frank revised his earlier ideas. The kind of privacy that divided houses into small spaces like cells of a penal institution seemed no longer valid. Now he was thinking in terms of one large room zoned for various activities. Having screens rather than partitions would give a greater sense of freedom. The kitchen area, set apart like a laboratory, would have a flue to carry away odors.

When Herbert Jacobs, a young journalist, conferred with him in 1937 about a house he wanted to build at Westmoreland, near Madison, Wright decided to make this a sort of pilot project for low-cost houses. He wanted to prove that with a modest sum, fifty-five hundred dollars in this case, one could come up with a beautiful product. To get rid of complications in construction and eliminate labor costs as far as possible he and Mr. Jacobs agreed on prefabricated plywood walls. Through use of three thicknesses of boards, the walls would be high in insulating value, would be vermin-proof, almost fireproof.

In the interest of good architecture at minimal expense, the Jacobses consented to substitute a carport for a garage and to forego a basement. Use of wood for the interior with only a coat of resinous oil would impart warmth and charm, yet make plaster or paint unnecessary. Korean heating, a gravity type not to be confused with radiant, would eliminate radiators.

Essentials as far as the family were concerned were a big living room with a fireplace, an adjacent dining and cooking space, two bedrooms, a workshop, a bath, and as much vista and garden as possible. The house turned its back on the street. Because Wright had economized on other materials he could splurge on plate glass windows. Conveying a sense of space, light, and individuality, the dwelling was proof that a modestly priced house could be built without resorting to cheap expedients or standardization.

Others could be built for a like sum, but not without an architect's supervision, which would mean additional cost. In this instance Wright's fee of five hundred dollars had been included in the fifty-five hundred.

When not supervising construction of the Johnson Building or houses, Wright was designing Taliesin West, where the Fellowship could make its winter home. He had found a mesa in Paradise Valley, twenty-six miles from Phoenix, that he considered an ideal location. The only road into it was little more than a trail, but it could be improved. He'd been inspired by the character and beauty of the place, and there'd be plenty of sunburned rocks available for construction. Through a part-lease, part-purchase plan, Wright had acquired eight hundred acres.

The buildings, he decided, would be somewhat like those in the Ocatilla Camp. Good architecture should always accentuate the characteristics of the landscape. On the desert lines were savage, sharp and clear: Taliesin West must belong to the cacti and barren rocks. Because Arizona sunlight is strong, a building's surface should break it up, drink it in.

Paradise Valley was even more beautiful than he'd remembered it, Wright thought, as he stood on Maricopa Mesa looking down at the sand rolling off like a dead sea toward McDowell Peak.

Taliesin West, Arizona

From this vantage point sunrises and sunsets would be magnificent.

To build Taliesin West, stone, redwood trusses, stout canvas had to be hauled over the inadequate trail. For the waist-high walls, apprentices picked up desert stones—gold, green and rose quartz. These were placed in wooden forms and bound together by concrete to produce a bold, coarse texture. When completed, the massive walls had a reassuring solidity and looked as if they'd been part of the desert for hundreds of years.

The light framework for the canvas roofs was of redwood with rafters above the canvas instead of below. On warm days the top and sides of the buildings were left open, inviting birds to fly clear through.

Natives had warned that Wright wouldn't be able to get an adequate water supply, but the well drillers he brought in hit an abundance of water at a depth of four hundred and eighty-six feet. The road continued to be a problem. Although apprentices improved it, a heavy rain would leave it knee-deep in water, marooning the Fellowship. Occasionally sandstorms cut the mesa off from the outside world. But Frank had no regrets at having located here. He found the shimmering sand and the cactus-dotted hills stimulating, and yet he felt at peace.

Now that Walter Gropius had come from Germany to America to head the Department of Architecture in Harvard's Graduate School of Design, much was being said about the International Style. The functionalism preached by its adherents could not be a style, Wright asserted, for style must vary with the terrain and with the needs of the individual. And why adhere to formulae when nature's wealth of suggestion was inexhaustible? Develop techniques of your own, he urged his apprentices.

Geometric purity of outline with no ornament had become a fetish, he charged. The functionalists were right in their insistence that architecture must serve industrialized society but true ornament was the inherent melody of structure. Wright also quarreled with the International School for their insistence upon the use of new materials even when the old might serve equally well.

For the views of Mies van der Rohe, the Berlin architect arriving in this country to become Director of Armour Institute,

Wright had more sympathy. Mies was a guest at Taliesin for two weeks before taking over his post. He had been greatly influenced by Wright and sincerely admired the boldness of his views.

Independent in thought and action, van der Rohe had in 1925 founded the Zehner Ring, an architectural group formed to offset official prejudice against the modern movement in architecture. His buildings, including a pavilion for the 1929 exposition in Barcelona, Spain, had been outstanding. Now he too talked of organic architecture, of indoors and outdoors flowing into each other. Wright introduced Mies at a banquet given in his honor by the American Institute of Architects at Palmer House, but was offended because speakers referred to modern architecture as if it were something coming from abroad, ignoring Wright's contributions.

About this time Wright was working on a unique project. Dr. Ludd M. Spivey, President of Florida Southern College at Lakeland, had asked him to plan their whole campus, which would ultimately comprise sixteen buildings. Since the site was in an orange grove sloping toward a lake, Wright immediately thought of a richly planted area that would be southern in feeling. His plan of steel-reinforced concrete buildings connected by deeply shaded esplanades appealed to Dr. Spivey.

Meanwhile the Johnson Administration Building opened with much fanfare. Newspapers headlined the event, movie shorts were made on the subject, newsmen broadcast it as "Unique" . . . "musical" . . . "a thoroughbred."

In all kinds of weather, Wright had made more than one hundred and thirty-two trips between Taliesin and Racine, a distance of a hundred and sixty-five miles, to supervise the building. Once he had come down with pneumonia as a result of overexposure.

But none of that mattered now, thought Wright, as he viewed the streamlined building that seemed so sure of itself. The columns that had caused such a welter of controversy were like graceful things standing on tiptoe. Throughout the building there was abundant outdoor light, with glare eliminated by aeroshades. When artificial illumination was needed, it came from lights in glass tubing laid in the walls of brick and red kasota sandstone.

Wright was pleased when he heard how the employees' morale

had improved after the company had moved into the new building. Some insisted that it was so beautiful that they hated to go home at night. Executives too put their stamp of approval on the structure, although they had been stunned when the final cost came close to four and a half million instead of the two and a half million Wright had given as an initial estimate. But the free advertising at the time of opening convinced them the building had been worth the cost.

During this period Wright was thinking and writing a great deal on architectural philosophy. Although he contended that he was more accustomed to saying things with a hod of mortar and bricks than on a printed page, he was never at a loss for words. In *An Organic Architecture*, published in 1939, he stated many of his basic beliefs. Organic architecture, he said, is natural architecture, true to the nature of the site, true to the nature of the materials used; and it is also honest, because it is planned for a particular place, time, and client.

In this book Wright elaborated on his concept of plasticity. Materials, he said, should seem to flow or grow into final form and the observer should not be conscious of cut, joined pieces. Walls, ceilings, and floors should become part of each other, and ornament must be one with the structure.

Despite greater acceptance of some of his ideas, Wright still incurred considerable hostility. His caustic wit and condemnation of sham culture did nothing to endear him to his victims.

In lectures and in releases to newspapers he frequently insulted civic pride. On one occasion he referred to Los Angeles as the great American commonplace. And when asked what improvements he could suggest for Pittsburgh his retort was, "Abandon it." Zestfully he tilted with conservatives, architectural committees and colleagues.

His tendency to disregard the contributions of other architects antagonized persons who thought Gropius and Le Corbusier were also original and sound. Publicly assuming the role of a potentate, Wright might fix with a baleful glance anyone who disagreed with him, but with apprentices, friends, casual guests—even reporters— he was tolerant, understanding and generous.

18 *WAR AND THE UNCOMMON MAN*

IN APRIL OF 1939 WRIGHT RECEIVED AN INVITATION BY WAY OF THE British Ambassador to deliver a series of four lectures in England at the university of his choice.

When Wright chose London University, The Royal Institute of British architects proposed joint sponsorship if the lectures could be given in their new building. As a preliminary the Institute invited Wright to become an honorary member and bestowed the Royal Gold Medal upon him.

With him to England went Olgivanna and Iovanna, now twelve. Even at Wright's first lecture, standing room was at a premium. Dignified and natty, he spoke without notes, obviously enjoying his subject matter.

Wright urged architects to go to nature for inspiration. They must learn to build from the ground—independently, truthfully, sincerely. Although he had been in England only a short time, Wright had sensed the tension and unrest engendered by fear of the military machine Hitler had built in Germany.

Wright was delighted at the high level of intelligence and awareness displayed in the question period after the lecture. He even relished the purposeful heckling.

In his second lecture he stressed the idea that the architect must be a poet and interpreter of his time, his day, his age. He also rebuked the English, once afraid of nothing, for having become timid. At the third lecture he showed pictures of the half-finished Taliesin West and described Fellowship activities.

Between lectures the Wrights went sightseeing. Iovanna was ecstatic over the castles, but Frank was disappointed at many of the historic structures which had been added onto and patched incongruously.

In the last of his lectures Wright emphasized the necessity for thought-built buildings. Science, he said, cannot save us. It gives us the tools in the box, but architects have to master a humane, cultural use of them. He declared that for London, as well as other cities, decentralization was inevitable. He appealed to architects not to think in terms of wealth and its power, but to get hold of something deeper and more substantial. Money could never be a substitute for ideas, he said.

Taliesin looked like a town in itself, thought Wright, when he returned to Wisconsin from England. Scattered among oaks, box elders, dark cedars, and white birches, the establishment now included, in addition to the main house and dormitory for apprentices, an exhibition room, drafting room and laundry; agricultural buildings, guest rooms and shops; studios for printing, painting, weaving, pottery, machine craft and model making. Taliesin had its own water, sewer, heat, hydroelectric plant and transportation system.

In the almost-completed seventy-board drafting room, apprentices ranged from young students just out of high school to graduate architects already established professionally.

Wright plunged into plans for private houses as far apart as Stanley Rosenbaum's in Florence, Alabama, and Bernard Schwartz's in Two Rivers, Wisconsin. When problems arose in the process of construction, Wright sometimes dispatched an apprentice as his representative. Because he had a tendency to think of clients' requirements in terms of his own needs and tastes, prickly relationships developed at times, and then Wright would have to go himself to soothe the house owner.

Challenged by the problem of putting quality into low-cost houses, he planned others besides the Jacobs house and became enthusiastic about multiple housing. For seven teachers at Michigan State College he planned "Usonian" dwellings to be located on a forty-acre tract, but when the group applied for a government

Schwartz House, Two Rivers, Wisconsin

loan the project was turned down. Reasons given were that the walls could not support the roof, floor heating was impractical, and the unusual design would make future sales a hazard. Later two of the teachers asked Wright to build a house for them at Okemos, Michigan.

Intrigued by Wright's philosophy and work, Otto Tod Mallory, president of Tod Company, visited him to talk over a project to be called Suntop Homes and located at Ardmore, Pennsylvania, near Philadelphia. Construction was delayed because the neighborhood vetoed an apartment house, but after the township board of commissioners saw Wright's model, they approved it.

The apartments were to rent for fifty dollars a month, which was very reasonable, since about forty percent of the furniture would be built in. Even before construction was finished there was a waiting list of tenants.

Wright eliminated paint, plaster and wall paper. The first completed unit was shaped like a four-leaf clover. Each leaf included six rooms, storage space, and a carport. In a unique room arrangement the kitchen was given a favored position. There were cantilevered terraces and a penthouse on the roof. Privacy from street and from neighbors was insured by high parapets. Suntop Homes made news and Wright registered a patent on the design.

In 1940 he completed the Ann Pfeiffer Chapel for Florida Southern College. White concrete wall perforations were filled with cut-glass jewels. The building had strong horizontal lines with accents provided through graceful, almost rose-colored steps and a tower ornamented by flowers and vines. Through the tower sunlight sifted into the chapel, where the pulpit seemed to thrust the speaker into his audience.

Between November 3, 1940 and January 5, 1941 the Museum of Modern Art in New York presented a comprehensive exhibit of Wright's work. Wright's plans, photographs, color transparencies and models ranged from the 1909 Robie House in Chicago to houses currently under construction and a Washington, D.C. project for hotel, theater and apartments covering a ten-acre tract. The superb models had been made by the Fellowship in a shop at Taliesin. Although power tools were available there, most

Pfeiffer Chapel, Lakeland, Florida

of the work had been done by hand. If the building copied was made of stone, each stone was represented in the model by a tiny piece of carved wood.

The exhibit depicted many of Wright's innovations, such as picture windows, and dramatized his ever-timely, ever-new patterns. Roofs might be flat, pitched, or planted with flowers, but each was appropriate to its environment and circumstances. The shapes of houses varied, but each one enclosed space as if it were precious. With every design Wright sought a better way to build, but never merely a novel way.

Wright had a corps of assistants at the exhibition. For visitors who could tell a cantilever from a truss, the show was a fascinating one, but some found the lack of explanations and jumble of diagrams confusing. Even critics could not fail to recognize that they'd seen the products of an eruptive, imaginative mind.

During these days Wright's thoughts were frequently diverted from architecture to international affairs. He had been deeply concerned by the outbreak of World War II in 1939, realizing that Hitler's fascist state constituted a threat to the entire free world. Wright's views on democracy were as colorful as his pronouncements on architecture.

Our forefathers, he believed, expected us to be truly individual, but the common man now allows mediocrity to ride too high. We should strive to be uncommon. Democracy should bring freedom for the individual to realize himself as a creative, free, unique person. But self-improvement is a condition of freedom, and it is only by discipline from within that man achieves true democracy.

As pressure increased for American entry into the war Wright in a letter to the editor of *Christian Century*, November 13, 1940, wrote that the bulwark against Hitler was not England or saving Britain, but "a free, enlightened, fearless minority having access to the best and bravest thought. We must," he said, "face the enemy on our own merits, not Britain's."

That winter Wright was, as usual at Taliesin West, where improvements went on continually. Concrete terraces, using the structure as a windbreak, afforded warm nooks for sun-bathing while sunlight and shadow provided ever-changing patterns. To blend with the desert and the staccato rhythms of the rock wall, Wright landscaped with yucca, prickly pear, mesquite and palos verde trees. There were gardens, a play court, and pools, including a plunge pool.

The main dwelling at Taliesin West was heavy and cavelike. In the living room, where masses of stone swept up to the sloping ceilings, there was a monumental fireplace, and it was furnished with deep-piled rugs, gay-textured fabrics, Chinese sculpture, ancient pottery. Flooded with extraordinary luminosity because of the canvas ceiling, the room had a seating capacity of seventy. A museum garden at the end linked the indoors with the outdoors, making the room seem one with the horizon.

The Taliesin West theater, in the form of a kiva, or Hopi ceremonial chamber, had a canvas top that could be partly open during performances. In the drafting room Wright discussed with apprentices the way a building affected the health, economic well-being, habits and thoughts of the occupants. A house expressing the integrity of its builder could bring repose to body and mind.

Music was as much a part of the Arizona Taliesin as the Wisconsin one. Wright contended that nobody could lead a full life without music. It developed a man's personality and helped him to achieve his goals. Wright's own tastes ran to the compositions of Bach, Brahms, Handel and Beethoven. Olga increased his appreciation for Stravinsky. Slim and smart despite graying hair, she continued to supervise the music for the Sunday night programs. Through subtle encouragement she did much to weld the Fellowship together.

In various parts of the country Wright's new houses were creating a stir. He had begun to emphasize hemicycle houses— buildings curved in an arc with long outer walls turned against the weather and inner, shielded fronts hung with glass. But Wright was incapable of devoting himself to one form: His untiring creativity demanded variety.

For Mr. and Mrs. Lloyd Lewis of Libertyville, Illinois, he put a house on stilts to take advantage of summer breezes and to afford a view of the Des Plaines River. When winter came, the floor heating didn't warm the house properly and the one small

fireplace at first refused to draw even though Wright had supervised the building of some three thousand that did. After double
windows had been installed and smoke rose as it should from the
balky fireplace, Alexander Woollcott visited the Lewises and afterward wrote to Frank, "Just to be in that house uplifts the heart
and refreshes the spirit."

For constructing the John C. Pew house in Sherwood Hills near
Madison, Frank relied almost wholly on his apprentices. Again he
stressed the necessity for gracing a site, not disgracing it. The
object, he told them, would be to change the site as little as
possible. As usual when breaking into the earth he taught them
to preserve the plants growing there in order to feature them or
their counterparts in the final landscaping.

No detail would be too small to merit precise, painstaking work,
Wright told his apprentices. Inefficiency could hamper the lives
of those who would live there. In the building nothing would be of
value unless naturally related to the whole in the direction of some
living purpose. As his apprentices worked with the tools of their
calling he made them conscious of the symbolism of the designs—
the square a symbol of integrity; the circle, of infinity; the triangle,
of aspiration.

The two-story Pew house with a view of Lake Mendota was
built of local stone and lapped cypress board. Supported by a
stone column at one end, because the site was hilly, the house gave
the impression of luxury but was economical in cost.

Wright often gave his clients a bad time. In the case of Mr. and
Mrs. Arch Oboler of Santa Monica, California, he told them at
their first conference that the house they wanted would take twice
the amount of money they had allocated. While the Obolers were
on a vacation cruise during construction, a radiogram came for
them saying that Wright had changed his mind and wanted to
substitute pine for redwood. Inasmuch as Oboler had already
spent four thousand dollars on redwood, he sent a strong reply to
the effect that he wasn't going to buy pine.

Back in California the Obolers were delighted at the first glimpse
of the house, but were later dismayed when Arch saw abandoned
in the meadow what appeared to be the front end of a building.

Taliesin West, Arizona

142   REBEL IN CONCRETE

The contractor explained that when Wright had inspected the finished front of the house he had ordered it ripped out.

After the main building was completed and occupied, the Obolers were entertaining guests at a barbecue one afternoon when a caravan of foreign cars swung into their driveway. From one of them emerged a figure in a cape carrying a Malacca cane. Wright stalked over to the redwood fence. Pointing his cane at it as if it were too loathsome to touch, he turned to his apprentices pouring out of the cars and ordered, "Rip it out."

Wright had designed the fence himself, but now had decided that the house would look better without it. In this instance, as in previous ones, he was undeterred by additional expense, loss of time, material, or even sacrifice of his own fee. If a thing had been done wrong, it had to be made right.

Dissatisfied because the Oboler guest house gave the appearance of squatting on the mountain instead of being one with it, Wright ordered ten of his apprentices to camp out at the site and do what was required to correct this. For the month it took to do the job the Obolers fed the apprentices.

Not all of Wright's clients had such expensive, harrowing experiences as the Obolers, but even those who did usually concluded their house was worth what it had cost. Wright's houses had a plus something, and in the planning of them Wright and his client shared moments of insight and beauty.

On December 7, 1941, Japanese bombers blazoned with emblems of the Rising Sun dropped bombs on the American fleet anchored in Pearl Harbor. The treacherous attack angered Frank, and yet it pained him to be at war with a country whose people he had come to admire and count upon as friends. He well knew that in time of war the destruction of public buildings becomes an objective. The Imperial Hotel had withstood earthquake, but it couldn't survive bombing.

19 *BUILDING BOOM*

A FEW DAYS AFTER THE JAPANESE ATTACK ON PEARL HARBOR, THE Congress of the United States declared that a state of war also existed with Germany. Wright knew what that meant for architects and architecture. With raw materials and labor diverted to the all-out defense effort, building, except for essential industries, would be virtually at a standstill. Young men who would normally be applying for apprenticeship training would be serving in the armed forces.

Several weeks later while listening to a New Year's Eve broadcast at Taliesin West, Frank was surprised to learn that His Majesty's Royal Gold Metal had been bestowed upon him by George VI of England. That in the midst of a struggle for survival the King would think of honoring an architect touched him deeply.

In January of 1942 Wright received a cablegram from the *News Chronicle* asking for fifteen hundred words of suggestion for the rebuilding of London. Repeated bombings of England had added force to what Wright had been saying about the need for decentralization, and that was a cardinal point in his reply. Among other recommendations was "No speculation in money, land, or ideas." In conclusion the cablegram read, "Don't grieve too much Britain. Empire not essential. The Empire of imagination is more enduring than any Empire of mere fact."

The cablegram was published throughout the United Kingdom.

The Fellowship was not so much affected by the war as might

have been expected. With apprentices coming from all over the world—Egypt, China, Palestine, South Africa—the number continued to increase.

When there weren't projects away from Taliesin there were plenty at hand to keep everyone busy—improvements on the buildings, farming, supplementary handicrafts, care of the grounds, model making. Almost self-nourished and self-sustained, the apprentices offset food shortages by filling the root cellar until it bulged with piles of potatoes, squash, beets, carrots, onions, parsnips and hundreds of quarts of canned tomatoes, beans, peas, fruits, jams, jellies, sauces, and pickles.

In performance of all duties, whether in the field or the drafting room, Wright stressed quality of workmanship, rather than quantity. Quality, he taught, meant individuality and was therefore difficult. The young architect seeking easy success through shoddy or superficial methods would betray not only his clients but himself. "I have seen the price you have to pay for success," Wright told them, "unremitting devotion, hard work, and an inextinguishable love for the thing you would have happen—love enriched with reverence for beauty and truth." That what a person believed in would happen, Wright never doubted. But success could never be attained by belief alone: it required interior discipline.

For assistance in Taliesin projects Wright often looked to Wes Peters, once a favorite apprentice, now a devoted son-in-law. For some time after their marriage he and Svetlana had lived away from Taliesin, but now they had bought an adjacent farm. Wes, with his generosity and architectural know-how, Svetlana with her charm and musical talent, contributed much to the Fellowship.

Despite the war the stream of visitors to Taliesin continued unabated. Whenever possible casual guests were served tea beside a fireplace or in the outdoor tea circle reached by a dramatic flight of steps.

A most welcome overnight guest was Alexander Woollcott. Although the square-faced man with a beaked nose and negligible mustache sometimes gave the public the impression he was a nail-eater, Frank knew his innate kindness.

For breakfast, served outdoors on a terrace to take advantage of sunshine and the flower-laden breeze, Alec appeared in dark blue silk pajamas. Also at the table, where anemones rested in a big, shallow glass bowl, were Olga, Frank, Iovanna, Wes and Svetlana, wearing bright slacks and blouse.

Interspersed with the conversation were the gentle tinkle of cow-bells and the yooo-ho-oo of peacocks on the roof. Olga, a gracious hostess, supervised the serving of Taliesin-grown strawberries in a Chinese celadon bowl, fresh eggs, broiled bacon, oatmeal that had cooked four hours in a double boiler and a pitcher of Guernsey cream to pour over it.

Spreading Taliesin-produced comb honey on his graham toast, Woollcott charmed the whole family with his wit. Teen-aged Iovanna was growing up, thought Wright, noticing her gracious manners and concern for their guest. After she had gone off to school and Wes and Svetlana had left, the two men discussed a wide range of subjects, with Woollcott, as usual, making brilliant, marvelous things out of the commonplace.

Refreshed by his friend's visit, Frank resumed work on a housing project for the government at Pittsfield, Massachusetts. Avoiding obvious standardization, he made allowance for plenty of yard space. Unfortunately, after construction was already under way on one unit, it was decided that only local architects could participate.

As World War II continued with its senseless destruction, he deplored the increasing curbs on individual liberty. Wright was saddened when news came that the Imperial Hotel had been hit by United States bombers blasting Tokyo. Four hundred incendiaries gutted the south wing, burning out one hundred and fifty bedrooms. The Peacock Room also was damaged. The rest of the building, although rubble-littered, was still usable.

Havoc caused by atomic bombs dropping on Hiroshima in 1945 added force to Wright's arguments for decentralization, a theme he made much of in his book *When Democracy Builds*, published the same year. In it he objected violently to current concepts of business, banking and finance that encouraged money grabbers and permitted fortune-mongers to enslave others. He also resented skyscrapers, slums, and centralization. Overpopulated cities and overdeveloped industries permitted domination by selfish, vested interests, he said. The solution he offered was decentralization along the lines of Broadacre City.

Picturing the ideals of early Americans, he scolded citizens of today for ignoring the spiritual aspects of life. With customary courage he outlined his dream for a truly democratic society and voiced an appeal for help in molding a world that would be a more honest and inspiring place. The reader was reminded of his responsibilities to others.

The end of World War II gave architects the greatest building opportunities in history. Although the United States had not been subjected to the immense devastation of the European countries, the national emergency had suspended most construction, except for defense purposes. During the unprecedented building boom that followed, Wright was deeply involved.

In 1946 at the age of seventy-seven he was working ten hours a day designing houses, a laundry, a research laboratory, and a hotel. At the various sites for his buildings he amazed everyone by the way he could skim through a mass of material and labor, poke at a thing or two with his cane, and emerge with a complete mastery of details.

Time magazine in 1948 referred to Wright as the most creative of living architects. Because of his success in training apprentices, now numbering around sixty, educators had become interested in his views. When asked what schools would be like in Broadacre, he outlined a plan for neighborhood schools with enrollment not exceeding forty children. Subjects taught would include music, poetry, drama, cooking, art, drafting. You can't substitute science for art, philosophy, or religion, he warned. Each school should have a garden space in which students could learn to live in love and harmony with nature. The teachers should be the best paid, best qualified, most important members of society.

Wright believed that students should be enlightened rather than conditioned. Enlightenment could come only through self-knowledge, experience, and an education on speaking terms with culture. Youth should also be given a sense of American freedom.

In 1949 the Board of Directors of the preponderantly traditional

Unitarian Church, Madison, Wisconsin

American Institute of Architects by unanimous decision voted to confer on Wright the organization's gold medal—the profession's highest award. To receive it he went to Houston, Texas, at the time of the Institute's eighty-first convention. For the award ceremony a thousand delegates augmented by guests and students overflowed the great ballroom in the Rice Hotel.

President Douglas W. Orr read a glowing tribute to Wright, calling him a titanic force in bringing new beauty and one who had moved men's minds and kindled their hearts.

Wright, with poise and dignity, but a madcap twinkle in his eyes beneath a halo of snowy hair, stood up to accept the vigorous applause. "No man," he said, as his artistic hands caressed the medal, "is not eager to receive the good will of his fellowmen. Here it is at last, and very handsome indeed, and I am extremely grateful." In a talk sparked by humor Wright reviewed his career, reiterated his disapproval of standardization, and made a plea for the individual true to himself.

With his capacity for prodigal variety, Wright had under construction in Madison a Unitarian church of airy grace. The church board had originally intended to build downtown, but Wright had persuaded them to go to the country. Walls were native limestone and the trussed roof covered with copper had a steep triangular upthrust not unlike hands folded in prayer.

At the same time Wright had the V. C. Morris gift shop under way in San Francisco. The façade was windowless, but subtle arches and a plastic bubble skytop gave the store grandeur.

Wright's inexhaustible flair for experiment was again apparent in a research laboratory for the S. C. Johnson Wax Company at Racine, Wisconsin. Planned to harmonize with the Administration Building built more than ten years before, the research unit was to connect with it by means of a tunnel. Fourteen stories high, with glass walls, it had floor slabs cantilevered out around a central core. In the laboratories, horizontal glass tubing admitted diffused light to working spaces. The central mass, housing the advertising and reception room, was spanned by a glass dome under a plastic shell.

Despite the demands made on him by various construction

Johnson's Wax Buildings, Racine, Wisconsin

projects, Wright still found time to produce a book entitled *Genius and Mobocracy*, published in June, 1949. Democracy, Wright contended, is in constant danger from a mechanized mediocrity. Average people tend to patronize the imitator because he is closer to them. Genius—defined as an expression of principle—is regarded as a sin against the mob, Wright declared.

In New York shortly after the release of *Genius and Mobocracy*, Wright was interviewed by Harvey Breit of the *New York Times*. The book, Wright said, had been the fulfillment of a promise made to Louis Sullivan.

Queried on problems ahead, Wright indicated that he saw only challenge and excitement. Committed to the idea that to make progress we must always be ready to change, his outlook on life was that of a young man.

20 *FOREVER YOUNG, FOREVER HIMSELF*

EVER SINCE THE DAYS WITH ADLER AND SULLIVAN, WRIGHT HAD HAD strong opinions on theater design. Once while attending a play he pointed his cane at the stage and muttered, "Anachronistic bosh."

It took a moment for those seated near him to realize that he meant the proscenium arch and not the play. His designs for the theaters at Taliesin and Taliesin West had been praised, but no one had ever requested his services in planning one. He was exuberant when he was finally asked to build a theater at Hartford, Connecticut. Hexagonal in shape, it had a workroom below the stage from which sets ascended by elevator. That the theater was never built was a disappointment.

Still interested in low-cost housing, Wright worked out a Usonian automatic house built of shells made of pre-cast concrete bricks grooved on the edges, which could be set up by the owner. The pattern, size and design of the blocks could vary to suit individual tastes.

Never a slave to patterns—not even his own—Wright seemed to have an inexhaustible power of creation. Every new site called forth a fresh approach. For a house on the promontory of Petra Island, off Long Island, he worked in terms of triangles in combination with a covered balcony overlooking the bay. The plan for toymaker Sol Friedman's house on a hill at Pleasantville, New York, was based on intersecting circles with a hat-shaped roof.

Wright was equally imaginative in creating furniture. Designs for tables included hexagons, triangles and circles that would mix or match in fascinating combinations. A cardinal rule was that furnishings should always be sympathetic with each other. He also wanted furniture that was substantial—usually hard rather than soft.

In 1949 Frank received the Peter Cooper Award for Advancement of Art. Lewis Mumford wrote of him, "One of the most creative architectural geniuses of all time—the Fujiyama of American architecture, at once a lofty mountain and a national shrine."

Educational institutions were acknowledging his work. In 1950 Florida Southern College conferred a Doctor of Laws upon him. On the Lakeland campus, still in progress, the chapel, library, administration building, and seminar rooms were already completed. The continuous esplanade connecting buildings, vine-covered trellises and flowers made the grounds gay and unconventional.

Wanting to make an exhibit of Wright's work widely available, Arthur C. Kaufman, executive head of Gimbel Brothers, Philadelphia, announced his sponsorship of a month-long exhibit at the store to begin January 25, 1951. From there the photomurals and models would be sent on a world tour.

Wright agreed to be on hand for the opening of the exhibit. Attending the banquet preceding it were distinguished Philadelphians, prominent artists and architects, the diplomatic corps, and representatives of the press.

The next day Wright appeared before the Philadelphia chapter of the American Institute of Architects. In his speech he touched on a number of subjects, attacking governmental policies and our lack of appreciation of our culture. Then breaking off suddenly he thanked the chapter for their medal, concluding with, "I accept your honor with the greatest humility."

When President Bendiner gave him the medal, Wright said it was beautiful, then handed it back, asking Bendiner to have a broad red, white, and blue ribbon attached to it so he could wear it. Everybody cheered as the luncheon broke up.

Also in 1951 Wright was awarded the Gold Medal of the American Academy of Arts and Letters, a selective group with only fifty members. Each must be "a creative artist whose works are most likely to achieve a permanent place in American culture."

Abroad, the Florentine De Medici Medal was bestowed upon him with much ceremony at the Palazzo Vecchio in Florence, Italy, and the Star of Solidarity was presented to him in the Ducal Palace, Venice.

Wright was not spending all his time receiving awards or writing articles, however. Concurrently with the travel and acclaim he was designing and supervising a variety of structures. Several of them were desert houses taking their place on the sandy soil as naturally as cacti. Another, built for Mr. and Mrs. William Palmer of Ann Arbor, fitted the rhythmic contours of a hill. The triangular shape of the living room was dramatized by an open terrace at one end.

One of the most remarkable houses he'd ever built was for his son David. The site was on the Arizona desert in a grove of citrus trees. Somewhat resembling a flattened snail shell, the house is raised on concrete piers to take advantage of the view. Circles of the roof, enameled with a coppery blue green, are like umbrellas. Dentillators on the edge drip water away from the walls during a rain and also soften the hard line. The plastic concrete blocks are expressive and decorative. A balcony sweeps halfway around the house. Flanking a breezy central court are shaded gardens and a swimming pool.

The house is entered by a long curving ramp bordered with flowers. Inside, ceilings and woodwork are a warm, brown Philippine mahogany. The house is air-conditioned, and the spaciousness of the desert seems one with the living room.

While the exhibit of his works was being shown at the École Nationale Superieure des Beaux Arts, Wright went to Paris. Not since the time of the painter James McNeill Whistler had any American been honored by a one-man showing. The exhibit and Wright's lectures while there were, in the main, given a favorable response. The newspaper Le Figaro stated that his work was stamped with "ferociously independent personality."

Wright's demeanor in public appearances was as unpredictable as his buildings. On some occasions he conducted himself with an almost cranky self-assurance; on others he was gay and debonair. When NBC interviewer Hugh Downs asked Wright, "What would you say is the greatest disappointment in your career?" listeners expected him to describe some project planned but never carried out, or a last-minute cancellation—San Marcos, for example.

Instead Wright answered, "Well, I think I touched on it a moment ago when I said that instead of emulation I have seen chiefly imitation. Imitation by the imitators of imitation."

Since his youth Wright had deplored the copying of medieval styles. Architecture must be a continuous rebirth, he had repeatedly insisted. Restatement was not creativity. Only when the architect escaped the paralyzing influence of imitation could he express beauty.

Pursuing this theme Frank was quoted in *Time* magazine November 9, 1953, as saying, "If honest seekers once mastered the inner principle, infinite variety would result. No one would have to copy anybody else."

In the drafting room at Taliesin he stressed the same idea, frowning on attempts to imitate his style, urging apprentices to find their own way of building. "The imitator steals twice," he warned, "once from himself, once from another."

From time to time Wright continued to denounce skyscrapers as "Gothic toothpicks, barbarous unnatural structures of verticality taking away breath, space, light from their neighbors. These modern 'steel Goliaths,' " he said, were not "ethical, beautiful, or permanent."

But he had also said, as long ago as in the Princeton lectures, that tall buildings were permissible when surrounded by park areas. If designed by men of vision they could be beautiful.

When Harold C. Price consulted Wright at Taliesin about a new building for H. C. Price and Sons at Bartlesville, Oklahoma, Wright agreed to design it if he could surround it with greenery. Bartlesville, an oil town at the foot of the Osage Hills in northeastern Oklahoma had a population of about nineteen thousand. Price proposed a three-story building. Wright suggested ten. In the end they agreed on nineteen.

The structure Wright designed had a backbone of hollow, re-

Guggenheim Museum, New York City

inforced-concrete pillars, each eighteen feet wide. These were set in a concrete platform twenty-five feet underground. Floors were to hang from pillars as spans hang from the piers of cantilever bridges.

Wright divided his time between Bartlesville and New York, where construction was about to get under way on the Guggenheim Museum, plans for which had been shaping up since 1945. Solomon R. Guggenheim wanted a suitable place for exhibiting abstract modern paintings.

Incurably progressive, Wright designed a building which in its main part was cylindrical in shape, almost like an upended egg with the widest part at the top. The outer covering would be winding bands of seamless concrete with marble aggregate facing, topped with a glass dome. Besides exhibition space there would be storage rooms, workshops, research laboratories, a conservatory and an observatory with a telescope.

The most revolutionary feature was a continuous floor surface consisting of a wide, corkscrewing ramp rising through seven stories on a cantilever principle. Wright hoped it would convey the quiet of an unbroken wave. There would be no stairways. Visitors coming to view the exhibits would take elevators or escalators to the top, then walk down the ramp past three quarters of a mile of wall surface where paintings were not to be hung, but would rest on prepared bases.

Ever since the plan had been made public there had been much caustic comment. The ramp might be suitable for a toboggan slide, but not for a museum; the pictures would appear on a slant, said the skeptics.

In August of 1953 Wright ran head on into building codes. The city's building department itemized thirteen objections to his plans for the Guggenheim. Over and over Wright had had to prove that his structures would stand up as planned. He was ready to do so again.

21 *TITAN OF TALIESIN*

HIS CALCULATIONS HAD NOT BEEN MADE ON THE CONVENTIONAL beam and post formula, but on cantilever and continuity, Wright explained to those questioning the soundness of plans for the Guggenheim Museum. High-pressure concrete would be rendered strong enough to do the work by filaments of pre-stressed steel, separate or in mesh. Anchored in bedrock, the museum would be as indestructible as a building could be made, Frank assured the commissioners. He did, however, backtrack in one respect, agreeing to eliminate a six-foot overhang that would have projected over the sidewalk.

With the building commission placated, Wright could proceed to other details. In the perforated marble floor of the vestibule, concealed air conditioning, working on the same principle as a vacuum cleaner, would draw off dust from the feet and clothes of visitors. This device would not only make maintenance of the building simpler but also keep paintings free from harmful dust.

Meanwhile the Guggenheim Foundation proposed making available to the public an exhibit to depict Wright's lifelong endeavor. Titled "Sixty Years of Living Architecture", the exhibit was to be an expansion of the one at Gimbels, which had since been abroad and would later continue its round-the-world tour. Assisted by apprentices Wright set the exhibit up with captions. Under the commentary, "Architectural corpses still encumber the ground," was a picture of a Gothic structure. Under "The space within is the reality of the building" was a picture of the Johnson Wax Building.

In addition to some thousand drawings, photomurals, and plates, the exhibit included a life-size brick and plywood mockup of a dwelling surrounded by grass and flowers. Called "The Exhibit House," it was meant to show how modern houses embody the principles utilized in Wright's prairie houses in the early nineteen hundreds—horizontal lines, a sense of space, the sympathic relationship between indoors and outdoors.

In October of 1953 the Guggenheim Foundation invited pressmen to a preview of "Sixty Years of Living Architecture." When the newsmen arrived, Wright, spare, erect, and rather awesome with his mane of white hair, was summoning workmen down from the roof to help him hang an eight-foot-square photograph of the now world-famous Falling Water house. With that done he patted down some earth around a potted shrub, and after flicking dirt from his hands turned to the reporters.

"We've been here all night for two nights getting the place in shape," he told them. "But it isn't work, it's a pastime."

Jauntily, with Malacca cane in hand, Wright piloted newsmen past blown-up photographs, including one of the Imperial Hotel, to a drawing of the H. C. Price Tower, which he had under construction in Oklahoma. "You see," he said, "it casts its own shadow on its own ground."

Twirling a long gold watch chain with one hand, he led the way out of the pavilion to the Exhibit House, where workmen were still carrying in furniture. Salesman as well as architect, Wright conducted a tour of the made-to-scale dwelling. "You see here the essential of what is now called the ranchhouse in modern architecture," he told the newsmen trailing after him.

By nightfall all exhibits were in place. Next day at the invitation preview, Wright appeared in a light brown herringbone topcoat worn like a cape over a golden brown suit. His dark, brown-striped tie was knotted into a loose bow. Seated on a built-in sofa in the Exhibit House with pork pie hat and cane in hand, the Titan of Taliesin conversed with a stream of distinguished visitors.

After a while a woman with a teen-age boy came up to Wright.

The young man, adulation glowing in his eyes, said he wanted to be an architect. What advice would Wright give him?

"Don't go to college," Wright shot back at him. "College merely starches you."

"Shouldn't he go to college for background?" his mother asked.

Turning to the boy with a stern look Wright said, "Get to work. If you want to be an architect you can't begin too soon."

In 1954 Wright was supervising projects at scattered points. He went to Los Angeles, where the municipal art society had a showing of his "Sixty Years of Living Architecture," received an honorary degree of Doctor of Fine Arts from Yale University, and published *The Natural House*. Once more he told of the struggle to develop organic architecture and made much of the nature of materials. "We have overrated what the head can do," he wrote, "and have given up those things that are leading lights in the spirit of man."

By late July, Wright had construction under way at the Guggenheim Museum. Temporarily settled in a suite at the Plaza Hotel, he dispatched assistants to arrange for a New York office while he talked to contractors and reporters.

One of Frank's pleasures in New York was occasionally seeing his younger friend Edward D. Stone, a highly successful architect who had designed El Panama Hotel in Panama City, and a number of other public buildings and houses in the New York area. He had also taught architecture at New York University and Yale and had won many awards.

The two men often dined together at the Colony Restaurant. Stone, a massive, disheveled man, was a striking contrast to the smaller, but regal and dapper Wright. Friendly, soft-spoken Stone possessed a personal magnetism that had always appealed to Frank, but architecturally they had, in the past, been at odds.

Once an ardent follower of the International Style, Stone was now crusading for a little more gaiety, ornamentation and warmth in modern building. The friends were in agreement that architectural design shouldn't be an assembly-line process and that the artistry of their craft should be maintained. "I'm a fall guy for beauty," Stone would say. "Without beauty you haven't got architecture."

Both men admired individualism and agreed on the necessity of organic relationship of building and site. Stone, by nature garrulous, was a good listener with Frank because he revered what Frank had to say about architecture and life. Wright voiced a hearty approval of Stone's work usually denied other contemporaries. He liked Stone's sense of proportion and his use of screened façades. His buildings had elegance and individuality.

Wright's concentration on the Guggenheim Museum was interrupted when in November the State Supreme Court of Wisconsin ruled that Taliesin was not an educational institution and was therefore subject to local taxation. It certainly was an educational institution, Wright argued, and the ruling showed a misunderstanding about what went on at Taliesin. He didn't mind paying the taxes, but he thought the court showed a lack of appreciation of what the Fellowship had done for Wisconsin.

Wright was then eighty-five. At that age most men would have been tempted to follow the path of least resistance, perhaps even to disband the Fellowship. In the past some apprentices after leaving Taliesin had become successful, but others had allied themselves to alien architectural philosophies or had surrendered their dreams. But for Wright the few who caught and kept a vision made the Fellowship worth the effort. Now in the midst of the busiest, most productive period of his life, he talked of moving his headquarters to the Berkshires or Adirondacks.

The governor of Wisconsin urged him to stay. That winter Frank took some time away from tax troubles, from the museum and Price Tower to relax at Taliesin West, where he could breathe clear air instead of carbon monoxide fumes, ride in his Jaguar, enjoy good food and private movies. But there was no longer a great deal of privacy. Both Taliesins had become almost a shrine.

Many who came were young men seeking advice on their career. Whenever he was asked what he considered assets for those aspiring to become architects his answer almost invariably included honesty, love of truth and of nature, sincerity, and fertility of imagination. To bring dreams into reality would require courage, ability to cooperate, individuality, joy in work.

More than ever Wright appreciated living close to nature. One side of the living room at Taliesin West had a canvas flap which opened to make the room and the desert one. The seventy-foot-long garden room had slanting glass panels facing cacti, shrubs, and flowers.

Because canvas lasted only about three years, Wright had, here and there, replaced it with occasional sheets of glass. Although the winter camp was not so self-sufficient as the Wisconsin Taliesin, it had a laundry, power plant, and a kitchen with facilities for feeding a hundred persons.

In the drafting room and in the fireplace room on winter nights Wright continued to instruct his apprentices. Taliesin West itself was an object lesson in architecture.

On Easter Wright and his apprentices put aside current projects and staged a festival. The day began with songs by the Fellowship chorus and an egg hunt. Breakfast was served outdoors on long tables decorated with colored eggs, brilliant desert flowers and miniature Japanese parasols. For the children there were separate tables with toys. The family, Fellowship, and visitors, swelling the group to over a hundred, ate, among other things, a traditional Russian bread, which had been baked the night before, and *paskha* made of cottage cheese, ground almonds, raisins, and egg yolks.

A short time after that Wright went east again. Prior to this there had been indications that he was mellowing with age, but a speech in Boston gave little indication of it. To the overflow audience he described New York as a city of prison towers. As for Boston, "Clear out eight hundred thousand people and preserve the city as a museum piece," he advised. Of centralization he said, "If it keeps up, man will atrophy all his limbs but the push button finger."

Somehow he found time to write *An American Architecture*, which set forth a record of sixty years of work. And the whole issue of *House Beautiful* for November 1955 was devoted to Wright, including pictures of his work, interviews, and statements

by and about him. One of the designs included was that of a house in a valley at Bethesda, Maryland, for his son Robert Llewellyn, a lawyer. Of stone block, glass, and Philippine mahogany, it grows out of the ground on a mushroom-like base of poured cement. The off-center chimney mass is circular. On the first floor a half-circle terrace opens off from the living-dining room area.

Details for the Price Tower consumed much of Wright's time, but the building was the culmination of a long-term dream. The building had both office and dwelling sectors, for which there were separate entries and self-service elevators. There were also an auditorium and a roof garden.

In both office and dwelling units much of the furniture had been built in. Ceilings provided heating, cooling and lighting. Tinted glass and copper blades gave protection from excessive light or air.

The tower, visible for sixteen miles, had beauty of texture and beauty of form in the slender dignity of its concrete planes. Alternate parapets were stamped with a pattern Wright had designed. Between the louvers and parapets faced with blue-green copper, the soft-toned concrete and the areas of glass, there was a constant interplay of colors. No two facets were alike. In self-imposed isolation the tower soared proud and free against the sky. It was the tree that escaped the crowded forest, thought Wright, as he turned away from the almost completed building.

Price Tower, Bartlesville, Oklahoma

22 *VISIONS A MILE HIGH*

AT TALIESIN TWO FESTIVALS HAD BECOME TRADITIONAL, ONE Wright's birthday on June eighth, the other an end-of-summer festival. Each one had a theme carried out with the help of costumes, dramatics, decorations and music. Since everyone could sing, dance, or play a musical instrument, these affairs were elaborate.

In the summer of 1955 the festival theme was the arrival of Marco Polo in Venice after his trip to the Orient. The fifty or sixty guests invited for the occasion had a dramatic introduction to Taliesin. As soon as they turned off the highway onto the private road there was an acre of petunias that had been planted by the Fellowship. Massed according to color, the pink and purple flowers produced the effect of a tapestry. At the entrance loggia with its greenery, sculptured figures, and a huge Ming jar, Wright welcomed his visitors with beguiling charm.

For the pageant, apprentices had rigged up a Venetian-style boat which sailed on a dammed-up pond. Around it guests were seated in the midst of colorful balloons and striped Venetian barber poles decked with streamers. Wright, who probably could have been a great actor, director, or producer, was obviously enjoying the spectacle. When the boat landed, apprentices in costume disembarked bearing gifts, trunks full of fabrics, and plates of food.

To Frank the Doge, and Olga the Dogessa, the actors made presentations. Each male guest was given a silk scarf, each woman a silk stole, all to the accompaniment of pomp and ceremony. Then the pier became a platform for dances, music, drama, and spontaneous comedy.

After the program the apprentices went off to cook dinner while guests fanned out over the varied courts and flower gardens or mounted to the hill crown, a landscaped area with a stone seat beneath a clump of oaks. Wright, with theatrical gestures, pointed out objects of interest, such as the Romeo and Juliet windmill.

After dinner they all went down a road edged by torches to the theater, where each guest received a program on a scroll. Entertainment consisted of a playlet, Venetian dances, and music played on antique instruments. Then everyone proceeded to the pond, on which floated two thousand votive candles blinking like wingless fireflies. A display of fireworks followed.

The festival over, the Fellowship settled down to its normal routines. Never overlooking an opportunity to correlate nature and architecture, Wright on one of the customary weekend picnics took along a tray of seashells, which he made the basis for an informal lecture. There were many principles in sea life that could be applied to architecture, he told his listeners.

After showing some of the variations in shape and color, he picked up a gray shell. "Here's a sober sister." But it too had beauty and individuality. Human beings in planning housing should have just as much imagination. Picking up another shell Wright called attention to the organic structure, the integral ornamentation, the expression of the inner life, the natural form. All these principles should guide architects, he admonished.

His concern for building or for life at Taliesin never kept him from taking a keen interest in public affairs. Alarmed by what he considered an overemphasis on science, he warned educators that although artists need to utilize machinery and scientific techniques they should recognize limitations.

When the Arizona State Planning Commission in 1956 publicized a plan for a skyscraper-type building which they intended as a replacement for the old capitol, Frank called it a "dated New York monstrosity" and countered with a plan of his own, but the design was not accepted.

By August of 1957 the sprawling concrete Guggenheim Museum on upper Fifth Avenue was giving signs of things to come. An interviewer from the *New Yorker*, interested in workers' reactions, found out that men who often worked on buildings without being familiar with the architect's name all knew Wright, who checked on progress about once a month.

One brawny, unshaven laborer thought the project was screwy. "The whole joint goes round and round," he said. But another thought it was going to look "very, very nice."

The Guggenheim had not interfered with Wright's literary activities. In 1957 his magnificent *A Testament* showed him to be at the height of his creative power. The book would be valuable if only for its superb photographs and drawings—over two hundred of them—but in it also is the essence of a fascinating life.

To youth he said that the best young men too rarely seek to be interpreters of the poetic principle. Instead they set up security and social standing as their goals. He warns that success in architecture takes depth of character and dedication to principle, to beauty, and to nature's way. Beauty he defines as "but the shining of man's light . . . the high romance of his manhood."

If his colleagues needed proof that Wright was still possessed of a daring imagination that made them wonder which way he would leap next, there was his Mile-High Illinois building, drawn and described in *A Testament*. Ingeniously conceived, this fantastic skyscraper design looks like a rapier thrust into the ground with blade upright. If constructed it would be five times higher than the world's tallest building.

Ten structures like his five-hundred-and-twenty-eight-story sky city could take care of the office staff of all New York, Wright claimed. This in turn would permit the construction of parks and play areas where there are now unsightly business districts.

Architects, office workers, maintenance crews and firemen saw in the idea what looked to be insoluble problems in connection with entrance, exit, safety, rigidity, and operational procedures, but Wright had answers to every objection. Building weight could be distributed around a deep-sunk tripodal tap root. From this would rise a rigid, reinforced concrete spine with floors cantilevered to it like ribs. These supporting slabs would be of special high-tension steel and concrete. Exterior wall screens of glass and gold-colored metal would be suspended from the edges of the steel cores. As it rose, the building would diminish in circumference.

The treelike structure would be light, but not at all rickety; and because it would be tensile and in equilibrium at all points there would be no sway, not even at the peak. Divided into four sections, it would be reached by four entrances via four-lane approaches. There would be decks for a hundred and fifty helicopters and parking for fifteen thousand automobiles. All utilities, heat, air conditioning, and plumbing would be installed in a hollow interior spine.

Since cables could not be relied upon to lift elevators the distance of a mile, Wright envisioned tandem cars propelled along ratchet tracks by electricity generated from atomic fuel. The capacity of each elevator would be a hundred persons, and there would be non-stop service to the upper floors. For emergencies special cars would be standing by. Cost would be up to perhaps a hundred million dollars, but that is only about half of what would be required to house the skyscraper's capacity of one hundred thirty thousand employees in scattered buildings.

From designing a space-age building Wright could turn to rustic chores, a musicale, or an appearance on television with equal gusto. An honored guest at the Spring Green, Wisconsin, Centennial, he appeared full of vigor and faith in the future.

Reporters coming to Taliesin at intervals for material for feature articles for newspapers or magazines would find Wright in the drafting room drawing with a firm, steady hand or supervising almost seventy apprentices who in 1957 had come from all over the United States, from Hawaii, China, Canada, Egypt, Greece, India, Italy, Holland, Japan, Mexico, and Venezuela.

The visitor might be invited to pore over drawings for a dwelling, a synagogue, or a cultural center for Baghdad. Wright had gone there to confer with the King of Iraq on plans for a university, civic center, opera house, art gallery, and a garden-covered island on the Tigris. Comfortably financed by revenues from oil, the King of Iraq was liberal in his cash allowances.

From the Baghdad project Wright might shift the interviewer's attention to the small country schoolhouse he had designed and was building only a few miles from Taliesin or plans for a Christian Science church at Bolinas, California. Interested in religious edifices high in imaginative expression, he had set new trends with his First Unitarian Church in Madison, the chapel for Methodist Florida Southern College, and the Beth Sholom Synagogue in Philadelphia.

In addition to drafting-board projects, Wright might discuss with his visitor anything from television to his strawberry crop or a flight to California to launch a civic center project for Marin County.

When one reporter commented on the demands made by fame, Wright quipped, "I don't mind the fame, but I hate the notoriety."

When an architectural storm broke over Congressional proposals to extend the east front of the Capitol in Washington, D.C., to provide office and corridor space for members of Congress, Wright was among those opposed. He characterized the face-lifting project as "absolutely profane."

From his crusade for the Capitol, Wright turned once more to housing. He had favored low-cost multiple dwellings, but not standardized urban apartment developments, which he called "sanitary slums." Still a bitter critic of conformity, in a news story out of Phoenix he launched a new attack on what he called "thousands of little housing communities lined up picture window to picture window where you can hear papa spanking the baby next door." He urged home buyers to buy privacy as well as a house.

Later the peppery patriarch, addressing students at the Massachusetts Institute of Technology, said the very words "housing project" had an evil sound. He also commented on the free city, "the city democracy has not designed as yet." Of freedom, he said, "There is no freedom without conscience."

During the question period a student asked, "What do you think of our auditorium?"

Wright cast a glance around the room where he was speaking, which had been designed by Eero Saarinen, and said, "I don't think of it."

Students laughed uproariously.

Beth Sholom Synagogue, Philadelphia, Pennsylvania

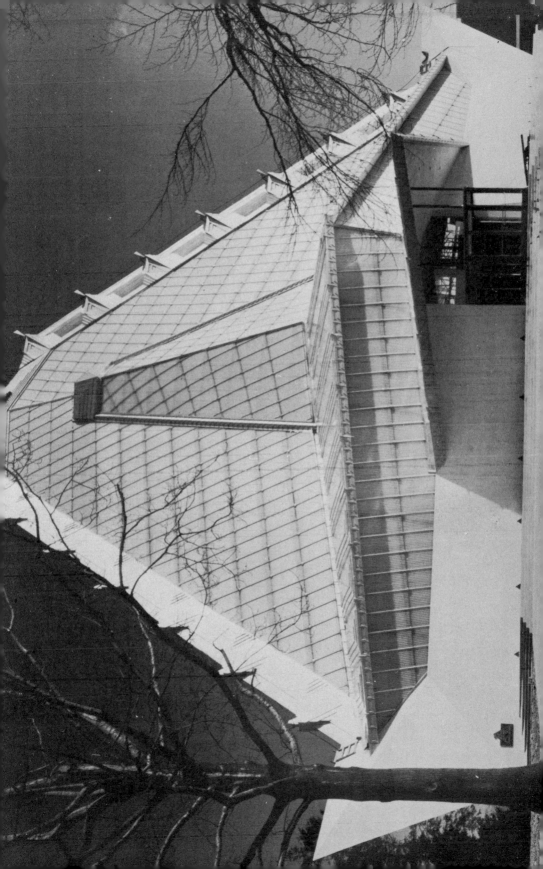

The fall of 1958 was a busy one for Wright. While in the East to supervise the Guggenheim Museum, he made many public appearances, including an address at the International Institute of Contemporary Art. Next day, interviewed by Henry Brandon, Washington correspondent for the *Sunday Times* of London, he said he thought people were waking up to architecture of our own. But he also added that many so-called modern architects built facades that looked as if wallpaper had been hung over the front of the building.

A tribute was accorded to Wright's work in a poll conducted by *Time* magazine. In it five hundred architects were asked, "From the lowly wigwam to the Manhattan ziggurat, what are the Seven Wonders of American architecture?"

Eero Saarinen's General Motors Technical Center in Detroit and Rockefeller Center, joint product of a task force of architects, tied for first place. Next came Lever House designed by Gordon Bunshaft. Completed in 1952, the dramatic tower of green glass rises from a plaza on Park Avenue in Manhattan.

But in the seven Wright had three entries. One was the earth-hugging Robie house with free-running cantilevers, nicknamed the Battleship. Long an architectural landmark in Chicago, it had recently been handed over to the National Trust for Historic Preservation for use as a library of organic architecture and also as headquarters for the American Association of Architecture, with membership open to anyone interested in architecture as an art.

Also included in the Seven Wonders were the S. C. Johnson headquarters in Racine, with its famous mushroom columns, and the Falling Water house. The other non-Wright building named was the Adler-and-Sullivan-designed Carson Pirie Scott department store of Chicago.

Although the Guggenheim Museum was not yet completed, it was among the runners-up.

A few days after publication of the results of *Time's* poll in an issue of September 29, 1958, the outspoken Wright made headlines in Chevy Chase, Maryland, a fashionable suburb of Washington, D.C. At a community improvement dinner he shocked his listeners with, "Chevy Chase is a blighted area." Costly houses were too close together, he elaborated. "Herding" took all the beauty out of things. After a few more words he put on his black pork pie hat and said, "I think I've carried this far enough. My bedtime is nine o'clock and it must be past that by now, and I'm going away."

Twenty-four hours later he was back in the good graces of residents of Washington, D.C., including Chevy Chase, when at Lisner Auditorium he offered to design a multi-million-dollar national cultural center authorized by the eighty-fifth congress. His statement was met by a burst of applause. A fine arts committee set up to direct the center promptly accepted Wright's offer to submit a preliminary sketch.

By the end of 1958 the Guggenheim Museum stood almost ready to open. The main face of the circular structure on the Eighty-eighth street side had no ornamentation, but the aggregate of white cement and white marble glistened in the sun. Stories curving outward as they rose to the domed top had almost the effect of a temple.

Not at all similar to buildings surrounding it, the Guggenheim aroused much comment. Detractors called it a concrete ice cream cone or a silo for art. But it was an attention getter, and many had high praise for it. Wright's comment was, "It says we are through with the past and aiming for the better things of life."

In that sense the Guggenheim Museum symbolized Wright himself. At eighty-nine he was still designing, thinking, and throwing out challenges. Early in 1959 his book *The Living City*, a rewriting and expansion of *When Democracy Builds*, was released. His ideas for decentralized cities to fit the individualism that should be recognized in a democracy, cities in which man and nature would remain in contact, were more idealistic than practical. But too many urban developers have pressured us into stopgap planning. We need the mile high visions of an architect like Frank Lloyd Wright.

23 *WHAT A MAN DOES, THAT HE HAS*

WORKING WITH APPRENTICES WRIGHT FREQUENTLY POINTED TO ONE of the inscriptions on the drafting room wall at Taliesin—"What a man does, that he has."

His own doing—over six hundred and fifty buildings of diverse materials, styles, and uses—indicate that he had much. Many factors entered into this spectacular total. There was, of course, his mother's sensitivity to art, her dream that her son would be an architect. Through her instruction and use of the Froebel gifts, Frank became aware of the rhythmic structure in nature and learned to look for the pattern of construction in everything he saw. From his father came the training that enabled him to appreciate the relationship between structures of stone and edifices of sound.

Farm experiences helped develop an unshatterable vitality, capacity for sustained work, and an optimistic outlook. Closeness to nature heightened his appreciation for form and color, and spurred him on a quest for the inner reality of things.

The good books to which Frank had access influenced him, especially Victor Hugo's *Notre Dame*, which affected the sense of art he had been born to live with. It seems as if everything in his environment conspired to push him toward architecture, including the collapse of the capitol at Madison, which time and again deterred him from having anything to do with shoddiness.

Early in his career Wright realized that to reach the pinnacle of success requires not only persistence but a willingness to keep on growing and improving. Recognizing the law of change as "truth's great eternal," he was in his search for varied uses of materials and for new techniques of expression tireless in experimentation. But because he saw the studying, struggling and retesting as part of a great becoming, he found joy in it.

The drive that comes from singleness of purpose, the sense of adventure in all work, carried him through difficulties. While wrestling with a plan he had the sense of something about to be born, something that might live as a message of hope. In faith, but with a little fear too, he would begin to draw. Then came hours of alternate self-questioning and anticipation. A small-scale drawing, then a larger, and a larger one. One design, a dozen, and perhaps the dream still was not put down on paper. But there was the knowledge that he had a message, his own, and it could be captured. Now came the long hours of discipline for the imagination —days, nights, twenty drawings, thirty—and at last the structure would come through. The time that had been spent no longer mattered.

From the first project to his last one, Wright carried within him an indomitable ambition. When NBC interviewer Hugh Downs asked, "What do you consider your most satisfactory achievement?" Wright answered, "Oh, my dear boy—the next one, of course. The next building I build."

Wright could never have turned out the amount of work he did, often under terrific external pressures, had he not been possessed of an inner security. In the Taliesin studio a cast iron head of Buddha was a constant reminder of the calm he felt to be an absolute necessity in production of any work of art. But the repose he sought was never idleness, but repose in action, for Wright believed man possessed an interior guiding light. Man, he said, is too subject to his intellect instead of being true to his own spirit. It was Wright's belief that beautiful buildings are more than scientific—they are true organisms spiritually conceived.

Another factor in Wright's success was his individuality. Roused by imitations—because to him originality was a most desirable human value—he sounded a clarion call to imitate only the bravest and best. Even persons who criticized Wright's buildings admitted that they were unique.

Individuality got in his way at times. Outcroppings of egotism manifested in theatrical monologues, tirades against those so bold as to question the rightness of Wright, the tendency to discount the achievements of colleagues, engendered hostility and brought charges that he was vain, stubborn and bigoted.

To a degree his critics were justified in their comments. But part of the opposition was that encountered by any individual who dares to be different. Wright himself said, "The uncommon man—the one who is great and good and talented—is probably already unconstitutional and I suspect soon will have to sue for pardon."

Clinging to the knowledge that freedom comes from within, Wright was never deterred from his goals by censure directed at him or his buildings; but it frequently took high courage to stand alone against bankers, contractors, reporters and colleagues who misunderstood, maligned, or misinterpreted his ideals. That he was a man of valor no one can deny. Weaklings would have gone down in defeat confronted by a twice-destroyed Taliesin, financial reverses, last-minute cancellation of building projects, personal entanglements and stark tragedy. But Wright, relying on the inner light, came through with the conviction that in reality there can be no evil, since even a shadow is of the light.

Part of Wright's capacity for continuing creativity lay in his ability to put a current project aside temporarily and find refreshment in simple pleasures—hiking, swimming, riding horseback. He enjoyed both making and listening to music. On a shelf in his bedroom at Taliesin was an harmonium which he played with abandon and delight.

In these pursuits his mind often dwelt on analogies or ideas related to architecture, for such was his joy in it that it entered into his recreation as well as his work.

A major explanation for Wright's pre-eminence was that he thought in terms of service to society, not merely profit or fame, which he said will always mean more to posterity than to the recipient. It was his conviction that the true architect sees architecture never as a business, but always as a utility, and "his concern must always be for the heart of humanity." Architecture, the great mother-art, can give new resources for living happily.

Whatever Wright did, whether designing a Christmas card, a

desert camp, or a research laboratory, was done with a view to quality. As a result his buildings have been remarkably durable. His solid, substantial prairie houses have outlived fussy ones of the same period. Often his dwellings seem actually to grow younger and more beautiful with age.

Again and again Wright said in different words that what is most needed in architecture is the very thing most needed in life—integrity. It was his contention that what a man builds can never express more than he is. A flashy, dishonest architect builds that kind of building. An honest building will have no false façades, no imitation of the works of others. Wright's buildings showed his admiration for original, honest work. They will not last forever, but their principles will—structural truth and organic engineering.

"Integrity," said Wright, "is a quality within and of a man. The individual has to know what it is, how to stay with it, how to live according to it." His idea of what constitutes integrity did not always tally with public opinion, but respect is due him for the way he stuck to his ideals.

In response to those who would say to him, "That's beautiful, but it isn't practical," his answer was that only the beautiful is practical. He urged young people to learn to recognize beauty in daily life, to cherish it. Furthermore, he admonished them, "To achieve the superior you must first refuse to accept the inferior. Look for the light and you won't dwell in darkness. You will then bring out something in yourself which is both practical and beautiful."

Frank Lloyd Wright, for whom the search for the beautiful was the greatest goal in life, died April 9, 1959. Behind him he leaves buildings that speak as poetry to the soul. Through his remarkable talent for blending machine-age materials with nature's living forms, he achieved a record unsurpassed in architectural history. Wright never thought of himself as a teacher, because he believed art could not be taught. He did admit to being an exemplar, and his leaping imagination had an influence on the builders of buildings that was international in scope. The words as well as the works of this uncommon man are destined, like a pebble cast into a placid pool, to set up reactions that will ripple off into the far reaches of eternity. Wright's genius will live forever.

INDEX

ABOUT THE AUTHOR

Aylesa Forsee writes: "While teaching in high schools and universities and acting as counselor at a Y-Teen Camp, I became deeply interested in teen-agers and their potentialities. It was inevitable after exchanging teaching for writing that I should put out a book which I hope will challenge some who read it to build the kind of life they dream about. I am not one of those writers who can point with pride to a novel or play penned at a tender age, having come into writing the long way round."

During Miss Forsee's childhood, spent mostly in Brookings, South Dakota, where her father was a physician, favorite pastimes were music, winter sports, Girl Scouting, camping and reading. Violin was her great love, but a late start made a musical career impractical. So at South Dakota State College she majored in science and social science, later picking up a Bachelor of Music degree at the MacPhail School of Music and a Master of Arts degree at the University of Colorado. Sandwiched in with teaching in Minnesota was participation in the Rochester Civic Symphony and the Duluth Symphony.

Miss Forsee's present home is in Boulder, Colorado, where she takes time out from her writing to go picnicking and camping in the Rockies and pursues her musical interest by playing in the Boulder Philharmonic Orchestra.